My Fight With God

FOREWORD BY:

Dr. Marilyn "M.E." Porter
&
Mr. Tamon Pearson

Ms. Jennifer Pink

Pearly Gates Publishing LLC, Houston, Texas

My Fight With God

Copyright © 2016
Ms. Jennifer Pink

All Rights Reserved.
No portion of this publication may be reproduced, stored in any electronic system, or transmitted in any form or by any means (electronic, mechanical, photocopy, recording, or otherwise) without written permission from the publisher. Brief quotations may be used in literary reviews.

Verses marked ESV, MSG, NIV, and NLT are used by permission from Zondervan via Biblegateway.com.

Cover Design by Larry Bruyninckx of Los Angeles, CA

ISBN 13: 978-1945117107
ISBN 10: 1945117109
Library of Congress Control Number: 2016941040

For information and bulk ordering, contact:
Pearly Gates Publishing LLC
Angela R. Edwards, CEO
P.O. Box 62287
Houston, TX 77205
BestSeller@PearlyGatesPublishing.com

What Others Are Saying

"When I see Ms. Jennifer Pink, I am always inclined to celebrate **MOTHERHOOD**. *PINK* reminds me of the joy of being a mom – yes, even being a **SINGLE** mom."

~ M.E. Porter, The Soul Shifter
CEO & Founder of The Brand ME and M.O.M.M.

* * *

"The little girl inside the box **THRIVES** to be the woman outside the box with no walls or barriers. **THRIVE** to be **BETTER**, not **BITTER**. *YOU* inspired me to be better than before. I love your mission!"

~ Anjanette Robinson

* * *

"*My Fight With God* will change the way you see God's plan for your life."

~ Lady Stephanie Newells, Relationship Central

* * *

"Because I am the leader of the Single Moms Who Pray Ministry, I was sent an early copy of excerpts for *My Fight With God*. Baby, let me tell you! I barely made it through the first excerpt titled "Josiah"! I felt her pain. I felt her thoughts. I felt HER. To read how she felt the way she did and not even know that's what she was going through hit me in my heart. Then I read the second excerpt titled "Ruth", and my heart was filled with peace. I was able to learn more about my friend, but it has also made me think about myself and what I am willing to do to learn from the example that Ruth laid before us."

~ Keah Danniell

"Ms. Jennifer Pink is an inspiration simply by being herself. The sharing of her personal journey invites others to share their experiences. She has opened the door for women across the nation to open up and let go of their hurts and frustrations in order to draw closer to the One who heals all. Ms. Pink feeds my spirit and challenges me to embrace God's plan. For that, I am grateful."

~ *Crystal McKinley*

* * *

"Ms. Jennifer Pink is a phenomenal woman standing in boldness and walking in her truth. She shares her story with great conviction. Through her transparency, she is able to encourage other women to not just survive, but to THRIVE! She is passionate about helping other women and exudes the light of Christ while doing it! Ms. Pink is unapologetic about her journey and is the Sage in her own right. God has carried her to great lengths, and I know this is just the beginning of her journey. Her fight was not in vain. She is now walking in victory because of God's grace. What a blessed woman of God!"

~ *Jonaee Coffey*, The Purpose Propeller
Founder & CEO of Propel to Purpose,
The Generation Uplift Foundation, Inc., and Coffey & Biz

"Not often in life do we come across people who give off the intense vibe of greatness with every aspect of their being, from the heart to the soul, and all the filters of the conscious mind. Well, Ms. Jennifer Pink is one of those people. Through her continuous hard work and her struggles, she has prevailed and brought to life a movement that will stand the test of time and change the lives of many. I am proud to know Ms. Pink. Daily, I am in awe of her dedication. She is a true example of what ambition, drive, and courage represent."

~ Israel McGhee
The McGhee Experience

* * *

"Ms. Jennifer Pink, the Single Mom Mentor, has been put here on Earth to help single mothers like me be better and to THRIVE beyond measure. Meeting her has been a true blessing in my life because she has created a platform that allows women of a like walk to embrace who they are, speak their truth, and forgive themselves through it all. Jennifer has taken me out of my comfort zone, which allowed me to embark on a venture of becoming a solo mom entrepreneur when I thought it wasn't possible. Her truth has taught me that I am not alone. I am glad we have crossed paths and not only became working partners, but also friends. I am grateful for all she has done with and for me. I look forward to continuing this journey with her because I know GOD has a plan for her to soar!"

~ Janelle Lopp

My Fight With God

Dedication

This book is dedicated to every single mother who has ever felt like God didn't love her, couldn't use her, and was ashamed of her sin.

I've been there. I've felt that. I fought God on His truth about my life. After these seven rounds and getting knocked down more times than I care to count, I have found victory! My deepest prayer is that you find it, too.

I pray my lessons help you navigate your fight journey and help you end your fight **TODAY**!

God loves you…and so do I!

This book is for YOU!

Ms. Jennifer Pink

Acknowledgments

There are so many people responsible for getting this book out of my heart and head and onto the pages that follow. I got emotional every time I have thought about writing these Acknowledgments. I hope I am able to convey how much the following individuals have helped, supported, and caused me to grow into the woman who was able to write this book **AND** the woman I will be tomorrow.

First, I have to acknowledge My JCrew: Jocelyn, Justin-Christopher, and Josiah. The three of you are my inspiration, my reason, my headache, and my heartbeats. I am nothing without you.

To my Mother, Father, and Grandparents: Who would have thought this would be my life? You gave me life. You raised me. You built the foundation. Now look at where God has taken me. I will continue Papa's legacy until I take my last breath. I will do what you have done – and even more – for my children. Thank you for laying the foundation that God built upon.

To Dr. / Bishop / Pastor and Lady Newells: Thank you for being my spiritual mentors, my big brother and sister, my best friends, my example, my strength, and my kick in the pants. To be able to go from running *away* from God, to coming to church, to sitting at your feet while soaking up your wisdom and discernment, to becoming your Adjutant – working alongside you and building up your ministry has been the most amazing journey I have experienced to date. Thank you for being ***The Incredible Bishop*** and my ***Stephie Cakes***.

To the men and women who have pushed me and wouldn't let me give up: I am forever grateful and in your debt. To the women who bestowed nuggets in my spirit and business that, at the time, I had no clue what you were saying or where it would lead me, look at what those nuggets have produced!

There are so many to name and I don't want to leave anyone out. If I do, please charge it to the emotions of writing this and not me.

Special thanks to Tamon 'The Complete Gentleman' Pearson, Patrice Washington, Denise Hart, Jasmine Powers, M.E. 'Soul Shifter' Porter, Kenya 'The Style Icon' Kirkland, Ty 'Swagalee' Scott, Sharmon Scurlock, Jasmin Allen, and My Kayin *aka* Kito Bell. I love all of you and am eternally grateful!

To Keah, Dominique, and Joy – my Ministry Team: Thank you for seeing what God put in me and believing that I was ready and worthy…even when I didn't. I appreciate your support and have truly welcomed and needed our sisterhood. Keke, we've come a long way. You've witnessed so many pieces of the journey I share in this book. To know that God is now using me to bring about change in your life and our relationship in order to bring forth a revolution and movement in His people is more than I can even begin to express. Thank you from the bottom of my heart. Ladies, I pray we always #*PraySlayThrive* **EVERY DAY!**

To my Administrative / Book Birth Team: Y'all ladies have pulled more out of me than I ever wanted to give. Janelle, you've propelled me and my business to a whole new level. I couldn't have done any of this without you. You've got me for **LIFE**! Takima, girl: You pulled, pushed, and helped me breathe during this whole birthing process. You were sent by God to bring His vision to fruition. From one single mom to another: You are doing **PINKTABULOUS**! Just keep following Him. To Angela *aka* Ms. Pearly Gates: You've always come through for me. You take my 50 million questions, my random thoughts, my *"I gotta do it my own way"* and just love me and stay tickled pink. I am grateful for you answering His call to do what you do so that so many of His children can share their voices with the world. **YOU ARE MY PUBLISHER!**

To the men who have propelled me to greatness: THANK YOU! Yes, even those of you whose stories I've shared in this book. Yes, even those of you who know you were wrong. Yep; even those of you who left me broke, busted, and disgusted. **THANK YOU!** Y'all are the fuel to my fire. You have molded and shaped me into the woman I am today. I wouldn't be ***Ms. Jennifer Pink, Single Mom Sage*** without y'all. Again, **THANK YOU!** I ain't *BITTER*: I am ***BETTA***, Baby!

Last but not least, to my Future Husband: Thank you for praying for me. Thank you for loving me. Thank you for growing through your lessons for me. Thank you for covering me. I feel you today cheering me on and smiling because of the steps I'm taking today towards my greatness. I can't wait for the day we become one and I can tell you 'THANK YOU' in person and say, **"I DO!"**

Foreword
By Dr. Marilyn "M.E." Porter
and Mr. Tamon Pearson

The very notion of engaging in a "Fight with God" has to come from a bold, strong-willed, made-up-minded type of chick – someone just like the one and **ONLY** *Ms. Jennifer Pink*! I am actually simultaneously tickled pink (*pun intended*) and Sisterly-proud of this phenomenal young woman. She has had the tenacity to take the very thing that so many women wear as a 'Scarlet Letter' – single motherhood – and built not just a platform, but a **MINISTRY** from it!

Having been one of only a few people in this entire world who had spiritual ringside seats to the main event boxing match between **"God – THE Almighty and Ms. Pink – The Single Mom Sage"**, I am over-the-moon pleased to see that **God – THE Almighty** won the fight and has taken His rightful position in the personal and business lives of *Ms. Jennifer Pink*. Because of His grace and mercy, that makes **PINK** a winner, too. There were no losers in this fight…except fear, doubt, and shame!

The Bible tell us, *"…wrestle not against flesh and blood, but against principalities, against powers, against the rulers of the darkness of this world, against spiritual wickedness in high places"* (Ephesians 6:12). It takes a huge dose of wisdom to recognize that the flesh in question is your own. Even so, you must push beyond that top layer (flesh) and move deeper into your spirit man (in this case, woman) and allow God to be the heavyweight in the fight in order that **YOU** might win!

My heartbeats are filled with the highest admiration and my lips speak blessings over your life, my courageous Sister-in-Christ!

> **Dr. Marilyn "M.E." Porter – The Soul Shifter**
> *Founder and CEO* of
> Motivational Outreach Ministers and Mentors
> Spiritual Life Coach and Advisor

* * *

Within five minutes of first meeting Jennifer, I saw two principles that dominated her life: her delicate vulnerability and her passionate desire to help single mothers.

Jennifer and I literally became fast friends. We both felt as if we had always known each other. As I grew closer to her, I learned about her horrid past, her rocky relationships, and her struggles with God – and I saw a person doing **all** she could to put her life into a comprehensive system…in spite of those things. There is a constant within that system: *Teach single mothers to stop surviving and to start* **THRIVING**.

As a three-time single mother by three different men, she took on the task of answering three questions so many of us refuse to ask ourselves about our shortcomings:

1. Why did I go through this in the first place?
2. What could I have done to prevent it?
3. How can I prevent these things from happening to anyone else?

My Fight With God

In order to answer those questions, Jennifer had to walk in the shoes of the biblical patriarch, Jacob, who struggled with God and refused to let go without being blessed by Him. Like Jacob, who limped throughout his life after his bout with his Deity, Jennifer had been scarred by the war…as well as blessed. *My Fight With God* is about that struggle.

Jennifer's vulnerability coupled with her delicate and almost childlike nature makes you want to shield her from life and protect her from harm. Her strength, her passionate means of attacking her life's issues, and her teaching and ministry towards women make you understand: You ***shouldn't*** and ***couldn't*** shield her – even if you tried. Her fight with God has made her better – not just for herself, but also for the others she seeks to help.

A struggle with God impacts the person who has struggled so greatly that they are changed forever. As you read these pages and embark on your way to the destination, you can clearly see who and what she has become. The struggle is relevant to the conclusion. *Please do not neglect to pay attention to the journey.*

Jennifer is giving you this glimpse into her vulnerability and passion. She eloquently shares where they have come from. Accept her gift. Meanwhile, prepare for your own struggles and the changes they shall bring to your own life.

Mr. Tamon Pearson
The Complete Gentleman
I.C.E. Ministries and The Real G Code Mentoring

My Fight With God

Introduction

God whispered in my ear, *"Write a book for the women just like you."* I **immediately** questioned Him. *"What can I give them? What am I going to say?"* He was silent. I went on to tell Him that no one wants to hear about my "ish"; no one cares about what I have to say. I tried to shake off His voice. I tried to ignore the calling He placed in my heart. The more I repeated the words He whispered to me, the more I knew I had to do it. I **had** to share my story, my heart, my issues, my faults, my pains, and my testimonies!

Still, I was scared. I was terrified! How could I do that? I mean, I am not even over it yet! I haven't made it to the other side! I'm barely making it day by day!

All I could see and think about was how much of a mess I was in. Slowly but surely, He showed me I wasn't in the mess anymore. I was growing! The more I reflected and the more I opened my mouth to share something with someone, the more I realized victory is not in obtaining any specific thing; victory comes from overcoming the battle, from still standing, and from still growing forward. No matter how much I had gotten knocked down...no matter how much they said I shouldn't be able to, guess what? I am **STILL** standing, growing, and achieving new heights that I never even knew existed!

The more I wrote, the more I felt *FREE*. The closer I hung onto His Word and His promises, the more I realized how much I had grown and was continuing to grow.

My Fight With God

Well, *My Fight with God* is the book He asked me to write. My obedience took several years, but I actually did it. I've heard His voice several times during this process. I've felt His hands steadying my hands. I've felt His soft kisses on my forehead while telling me, *"Well done."* God has guided me through this entire process. Because of **HIM**, the fight is over… Or is it?

If you've **ever** been in a fight with God…if you've **ever** felt that He has forsaken you…if you've **ever** felt like your sin was too much, know that I've felt all of those things, too. You are not alone. I've fought all of those battles, and this book is all about doing just that.

God told me to be a mirror for His daughters. *"Allow them to see themselves in you so that they may see My power and their future in Me as well,"* He said.

I urge you to allow me to be a mirror into your life. Read this book. Read my story. Let God show you some things through me.

Table of Contents

What Others Are Saying iv

Dedication vii

Acknowledgments viii

Foreword By Dr. Marilyn "M.E." Porter and Mr. Tamon Pearson xii

Introduction xv

Round One: Why Has God Forsaken Me? 2

Round Two: Blame vs. Responsibility 14

Round Three: The Shame of it All 20

Round Four: *Josiah* - My Catalyst for Change 34

Round Five: Faith of a Mustard Seed 50

Round Six: Lessons I Need to Learn from Ruth 58

Round Seven: Who is Boaz? What Does He Look Like? 72

Round Eight: My Fight is Over, But… 86

Are You Ready To End Your Fight? 96

LET'S GET SOCIAL! CONTACT MS. JENNIFER PINK! 101

My Fight With God

Why Has God Forsaken Me?

Round One
Why Has God Forsaken Me?

I was 12 years old - at the beginning of my teen years. I had been to church. I even sang in the choir at my paternal grandmother's church…but did I know God? No. Did I **know** that I didn't know God? Nope. To me, God was that all-knowing being who created the Heavens and the Earth and…well, that's about it!

Well, something happened at the age of 12. My mom started going to church, studying the Bible, and working on her relationship with **GOD**. So, what did that mean for an almost-teen? It meant I had to do it, too! At the time, the relationship between my mother and me was rocky (to say the least), but for some reason, when she put "going to church" on the list of things I **had** to do, I didn't fight it or argue about it; I just went.

I began to study the Bible with some teens, young adults, and college kids. Through the studies, I began to understand the **WORD** of God. I was ready to give my life to Christ. There were, however, two problems:

1. I *mentally* understood God. My conscious was awakened and I was ready to do it His way because I knew that's what I was **supposed** to do. My heart, on the other hand, was unmoved. I had no heart-ties and no emotional connection to God: I only had those things with the *people* who were representing Him to me.

2. I didn't trust God's promises for my life and I didn't dare leave it up to chance. See, I was a virgin and had planned on waiting until marriage to have sexual relations, but now someone else was telling me I **COULDN'T** until marriage. *That* wasn't going to cut it.

Problem #1 took a lot longer to manifest itself than Problem #2. After studying the Word of God and realizing I was going to possibly remain a virgin forever (*I'm sure that was my self-worth issues versus what the actual Word of God said*), I took matters into my own hands and had sex with my boyfriend. We will talk more about my men issues later. For now, understand that I was 12 years old…and he was 21. After we had sex, I was satisfied that I had the experience, so I repented and then got baptized in God's waters…the ocean.

Now, for some reason, my mother and I both becoming Christians didn't wave the magic wand I thought it was supposed to. It didn't give us that glorious mother/daughter relationship everyone else had. In retrospect, it did little to change our relationship because neither of us ever dealt with the heart issues of why our relationship was so tumultuous. You may be thinking, *"Well, at least you were following God. Everything would eventually work itself out."* Not really. The truth of the matter is it didn't. I wasn't following God. I was simply being a good student, absorbing the knowledge being given and walking the way they said walk. Because my heart wasn't connected, I wasn't **really** following Him. That's likely the reason why my relationship with my mother didn't get better before it got *way* worse.

Round One – Why Has God Forsaken Me?

I was a devout follower for a little over a year. I didn't breathe, sneeze, or cough if it wasn't in the Bible. If you weren't following God, we had very little in common and you probably thought I was in a cult or a freak. My friends consisted of **only** the other teens in the church. The **only** boys I thought were cute were in the church as well and, of course, my mentors and role models were in the church, too. My whole life was surrounded by the church.

Now, hear me out: I don't think there is **anything** wrong with people heavily-involved with the church or the people of the church being an active part of your life, **but** if you're not building relationships with people outside of your congregation, how are you doing exactly what you were called by God to do? How many blessings are you missing?

I'll let that sink in a bit...

Well, the time came when I was tested. My mother and I were not on speaking terms. I was living with the young adults in the church, being as self-sufficient as a jobless teen could be. Then, I met some boys who were part of the church but weren't walking the straight line I was walking...*so to speak*. One thing led to another and eventually, I started having sex again. The funny thing is this: I don't struggle with sex when it comes to sin. I'm very clear that sex before marriage is wrong. My struggle is with *love*. I **need** love. I need to **feel** loved. At the age of 12 (*and for most of my life*), I thought sex **was** love. Love and sex had become synonymous in my life.

My Fight With God

When the news of my sin broke in church, the relationships I valued with the people more than God became strained. My foundation of who God was and is started to, in essence, turn their backs on me. No one was running after me screaming *"STOP!"* No one was taking the time to understand why I had sex. I had sinned. They could see I was unrepentant, so they pulled away.

After some time, I left the church **and** God. You see: If I had learned nothing else during my time in church, I learned you don't play with God. You are either for God or you're not. **There's no middle ground.** So, when I left the church, I left the majority of my morals and rules. I didn't call on God for a single thing. Funny thing is this: I left Him, but I now know He **never** left me.

After I turned my back on God, I relied even **more** heavily on my version on love to get through life. If I really, really liked the boy, then I had sex with him. If he acted like he liked me, I submitted to him. Of course, when I was going through it, I thought all of that was love. *I mean, isn't that what the world teaches?* When we have strong feelings for someone and we crave them, we have sex with them – and we love them. Boy, was **that** the wrong idea of love! Looking back on it now, I clearly see and understand on a different level the importance of that famous love scripture: 1 Corinthians 13. The part that speaks to the difference between 'love the action' and 'really loving' is the beginning of that passage.

Round One – Why Has God Forsaken Me?

"If I speak with human eloquence and angelic ecstasy but don't love, I'm nothing but the creaking of a rusty gate. If I speak God's Word with power, revealing all His mysteries and making everything plain as day, and if I have faith that says to a mountain, "Jump", and it jumps, but I don't love, I'm nothing. If I give everything I own to the poor and even to the stake to be burned as a martyr, but I don't love, I've gotten nowhere. So, no matter what I say, what I believe, and what I do, I'm bankrupt without love"
(1 Corinthians 13:1-3, MSG).

Just because I'm doing everything that those who love do and just because I am masking my actions as love doesn't make it love at all. Love is deeper than just being with someone, having sex with them, and heck…even submitting to them! So, what is love?

*"Love never gives up.
Love cares more for others than for self.
Love doesn't want what it doesn't have.
Love doesn't strut, doesn't have a swelled head, doesn't force itself on others, isn't always "Me first", doesn't fly off the handle, doesn't keep score of the sins of others, doesn't revel when others grovel, takes pleasure in the flowering of truth, puts up with anything, trusts God always, always looks for the best, never looks back, but keeps going to the end"*
(1 Corinthians 13:4-7, MSG).

I honestly believe if I had learned who God was and what love was from the beginning…if I had built a relationship with God… I would have never left Him.

My Fight With God

First of all, God starts it off with the hardest part: *"Never Give Up!"* Never say, *"This is too much for me to handle. I just can't do this."* That was enough to show me I wasn't loving anyone around me – not even myself. **Then** He goes on to say that I **should** care more about others than myself; I **should** be content with what I have; I **shouldn't** be proud, boastful, demanding, and self-centered. I should **never** get crazy angry, keep a tally of what all has been done to me, nor be happy when people (the haters) have to come back and need me. I, instead, should be **excited** about the truth – even when it hurts, accept people where they are and not change them, trust God, always look for the good in every situation, and (most importantly) don't look back, but rather steadily grow, change, and move forward.

The only reason I decided to write this book and relive my past is because I know there are other women – especially single moms – who need the lessons I've learned from my fight with God. If this is you, know that you don't have to fight Him. You are not alone. Learn the lesson in your similar story and start **THRIVING** just like I am!

Now, back to my fight with God forsaking and leaving me.

Round One – Why Has God Forsaken Me?

As I was on my own, I encountered many, many bumps, received *tons* of bruises, and flat out fell more times than I care to remember. When I got pregnant the first time, I almost went through the whole pregnancy with a prideful attitude of, *"So what! This is no big deal."* Then, as the due date approached, I began to weep and cry out to the Lord. I asked Him over and over again, **"Why is this happening to me?"** I'm sure God answered me then, but I was too busy **blaming** Him and being mad that I couldn't hear.

Two years later, when I had decided the man I was with was not the one, I began to date the polar opposite of the men I had dated before. I got pregnant again and that time, I got married. I twisted his arm into going to church and thought I was going to live happily ever after. After about a year, I think God decided enough was enough. He began to reveal how much of my marriage **wasn't** built for the happily ever after and that I couldn't twist someone's arm into following Jesus. Heck, I still hadn't built a relationship with the Lord myself, so I wasn't following Him either! My husband and I finally split and then God totally and completely left me, too. He left me all alone in this dark, crazy world to fend for myself. I definitely went through the Psalm 22 phase:

My Fight With God

"God, God…my God! Why did you dump me miles from nowhere? Doubled up with pain, I call to God all the day long. No answer. Nothing. I keep at it all night, tossing and turning. And You! Are you indifferent, above it all, leaning back on the cushions of Israel's praise? We know you were there for our parents: they cried for your help and you gave it; they trusted and lived a good life. And here I am, a nothing – an earthworm, something to step on, to squash. Everyone pokes fun at me; they make faces at me, they shake their heads: "Let's see how God handles this one; since God likes him so much, let **Him** help him!" And to think you were midwife at my birth, setting me at my mother's breasts! When I left the womb, you cradled me; since the moment of birth you've been my God. Then you moved far away and trouble move in next door. I need a neighbor. Herds of bulls come at me, the raging bulls stampede, horns lowered, nostrils flaring, like a herd of buffalo on the move. I'm a bucket kicked over and spilled, every joint in my body has been pulled apart. My heart is a blob of melted wax in my gut. I'm dry as a bone, my tongue black and swollen. They have laid me out for burial in the dirt. Now packs of wild dogs come at me; thugs gang up on me. They pin me down hand and foot, and lock me in a cage – a bag of bones in a cage, stared at by every passerby. They take my wallet and the shirt off my back, and then throw dice for my clothes. You, God – don't put off my rescue! Hurry and help me! Don't let them cut my throat; don't let those mongrels devour me. If you don't show up soon, I'm done for – gored by the bulls, meat for the lions"
(Psalm 22:1-21, MSG).

Round One – Why Has God Forsaken Me?

I went through losing my family, losing friends who were **more** like family, losing the safety net of my family, losing my grandfather, being homeless with two kids, not having a job (*and no real job in sight for over a year*), depression, and was filled with **so** much hate and anger. Then one day, it felt like God had decided I had enough and was ready to stop fighting Him. He turned it **all** around in just one day. He blessed me with a career, a home I could afford without so much as a worry, and (most importantly) a new outlook. I started to see for the *first* time how He never left me; I left Him. I saw how He had never forsaken me; it was I who forsook Him.

I actually started to understand that **everything** I had been through in my life I had caused. **Every** ounce of trouble and **every** bruise inflicted on my body was my fault. He *tried* to protect me before it all happened. He *knew* I was confused about the difference between sex and love. He *knew* I didn't understand what love was. He *knew* I couldn't make it in this cold, dark world without Him, and it was I who decided to not give Him my heart – to not open my ears to what He was trying to tell me. He gave me the foundation and I refused to embrace it. I know you're saying, *"That sounds good"*, but you're still not convinced. Well, let me give you an example:

As I told you, my relationship with my mother was tumultuous – to say the least. So, God brought us to a church that was founded on His Word: not pomp; not circumstance; not religion. He even showed me the difference between those who follow **God's Word** and those who follow the **Christian religion.**

My Fight With God

I remember it like it was yesterday…

Before I got baptized, my mom and I were discussing premarital sex. Now, I had known she had had it. I also knew that the Bible said it was wrong, but I still felt the need to discuss it. She took me to my father's family's church for some odd reason (*perhaps because I held all of my father's family and their things in the highest regard*) to ask the Pastor about premarital sex. Well, we sat down with this man (who I darn near thought could walk on water) and asked him about premarital sex. He looked at my mother and me in the eyes and said, *"Well, in today's time, it is to be expected…"* **That man had a golden opportunity to stand firm on the Word of God!** Instead, he taught me something else in that moment: He taught me to forsake God, to do what I wanted, and to blame it on the era in which I lived.

See, I **knew** the truth. I **knew** what God said. I **knew** His promises for my life if I obeyed Him. Instead, I allowed, sought out, and leaned on people and words that allowed me to bend God's instructions while pretending it was okay to do so.

Round One – Why Has God Forsaken Me?

Twenty years and three babies later, after tons of heartbreaks and too many emotional bruises to count, I decided to be honest, woman-up, and talk to God. I took responsibility for not listening to Him. I took responsibility for trying to bend His words and truth. I took responsibility for all the situations I had put myself in. When I finally decided to start being honest with God and start working my way out of the sin that entangled me, it was **then** when I began to see how He was there every step of the way. He prevented me from getting any diseases; He kept me from dying numerous times; He allowed me chance after chance after chance.

I began to clearly see how, when I got pregnant the first time, God spared me and tried to give me a chance at another life when I had a miscarriage, but it was I who darn near forced this life on myself. Now, it is I who humbly submits to carrying the burden. I am also fully aware that He will see me through. I can still make it to His Promised Land! I am also aware that all of the junk before I changed was just a precursor to the fight that He and I would face ahead, because from that moment on, our fight had **nothing** to do with other people…it had **everything** to do with Him molding and shaping my character into the woman of God He always wanted me to be.

My Fight With God

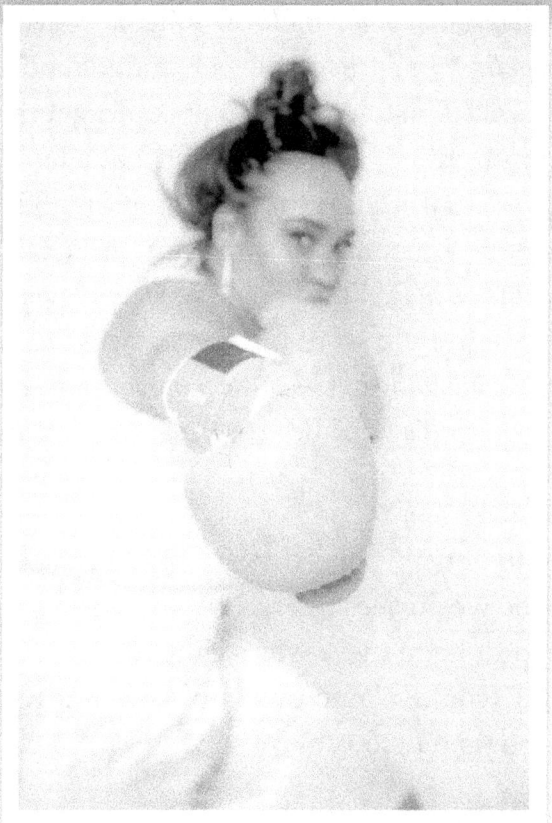

Blame vs. Responsibility

Round Two
Blame vs. Responsibility

Stop blaming everyone else and take responsibility and accountability for what you've done.

"WHY? But WHY? God, I just need to know... WHY?"

That's my daily mantra to God – just needing to know **why**. *Why did this happen? Why am I here? Why do I have to go through this? Why this life?* I just need a clear understanding of why. I mean, if He would just tell me why, I could get through it and we could stop fighting, right? At least that's how I see it. My need for the **why** of it all didn't just stop at God; I needed to understand why someone did something to me. *Why was I not a good fit for this or that? Why are people stepping on me just to get ahead?* Then a lightbulb went off and I started to ask **MYSELF** why! *Why was I allowing others to steal my joy and happiness? Why was I not doing it God's way? Why was it so hard for me to let go and let God?*

I had begun to notice I started to see my life the same way the majority of the world sees theirs. I began to see everything that everyone had done to me. I was seeing all the situations I was in and how I would blame everyone else **and** God. Before, I never took the time to look at myself.

Now, don't get me wrong: I truly believe I've been dealt some bad cards at certain points. I've dealt with some pretty nasty snakes and folks who meant me no good. I'm convinced God didn't protect me or catch me as much as I would have liked, **but** at the same time all of that was happening in my life, I was also being an active participant in the events as well *(this is my **TELL THE TRUTH, SHAME THE DEVIL** moment here)*. I was **allowing** people to put me in situations. I was **allowing** people to use and abuse me. I was waiting on God to do what I didn't want to do. Worse yet – and more often than not – I was holding on so hard to what they had done to me, I wasn't able to learn through the experiences to become exactly who I was born to be.

My biggest acceptance, release, and **WHYs** have to do with my family. Growing up, they taught me so much. They showed me what a family was. They educated me on generational wealth and cared for me better than I cared for myself. They were also jealous of the light inside of me. They hated the way I absorbed the knowledge given to me and was able to apply it. They resented how much they did for me and not themselves – even though I was a child and could not do for myself. Nonetheless, they saw it as unfair. They transferred their hatred, jealousy, and emotional baggage onto me so subconsciously, discreetly, and daily that I started to not have faith in myself. I was scared to be me because deep down, they taught me to be afraid…**of myself!**

Round Two - Blame vs. Responsibility

The worst part of it all was when I began to uncover and see all of those things. I didn't push away their hatred and jealousy. I actually embraced more of it because I dared to ask them, **"WHY?"** I dared them to own up to their actions and explain it to me in such a way where it would make sense. All of my questioning and needing of answers to my *'whys'* led them to push me further down, further away from my purpose, and further away from who I was born to be.

It wasn't until those around me decided to call me on the carpet about being unhappy, not seeing my beauty, and not wanting to shine full out did I begin to ask *myself*, **"WHY?"** When I started asking myself why I was unhappy, why do I not feel beautiful, why was I so afraid of doing what I know in my heart I am supposed to do…I got scared. I stopped fighting them and God. I then started uncovering the truth. Crazily enough, my *'why'* questions started to get answered!

During my third pregnancy, I remember asking God **"WHY?"** over and over again. All I ever wanted was to grow up, get married, and be an amazing mom and wife. I was born a mother and wife. It's who I am at my core. I was **furious** with God. *Why didn't He protect me from men who meant me no good? Why did he allow my frail, gentle, always-open heart to be stepped on and abused?* I remember wanting to ask the men I dated: *Why wasn't I good enough to marry? Why wasn't I good enough to be someone's wife for life?* The few men I actually dared to ask tried to give me an array of answers, but they **all** carried one common theme: *"You were too great/good for me"* or *"I wasn't ready"*. **What in the entire H-E-DOUBLE HOCKEY STICKS does that mean?** *How could I be too good for you? If I was too good for you, how could you discard me like that? Wouldn't you want the good thing for yourself?*

During my third pregnancy, I remember being so depressed and feeling worthless. I was so damaged and abused, I just knew no one would ever want me. All of that compiled into me being in a domestically-violent relationship. You guessed correctly if you thought, *"That led her to ask **MORE** whys."*

Why me? Why am I here? Why am I staying? Why can't I get up? The moment I stopped questioning was the moment I let go of everything and truly put it all in God's hands – which, ironically, was the moment I thought I was going to die. **That** was the moment I saw it all clearly.

Round Two - Blame vs. Responsibility

I had to take responsibility for my actions. I had to see what I was doing to myself. I had to see that I wanted the vision to come to fruition with such a great desire that I was willing to put anyone in the picture versus waiting for **the one** who was actually meant to complete my picture. I needed to unlearn **all** that was taught to me about love and who I was. I needed to learn how to value myself, how to see myself as beautiful, and how to love myself **first**. I had to stop asking everyone else *"WHY?"* and start asking **myself *"WHY?"*** In response, I had to learn to be accepting of the answers I would receive.

When you shift the blame and needing of answers to others, you give them the power and allow them to control you.

When you analyze yourself, take accountability for your actions, and see what you've done to cause the storms, the pains, and the situations you are in, **YOU** hold the power. **YOU** hold the key. **YOU** control the outcome of your destiny.

My Fight With God

The Shame of It All

Round Three
The Shame of it All

I used to walk around thinking, *"So what! I'm a single mom of three. Who cares? There are tons of single mothers. What's the big deal?* **Single mothers ROCK!"** Who was I talking to? Who was I yelling at? As I can recall, I don't remember too many people actually saying **anything** to me about the fact that I was a single mom. I received more stares and crazy looks because of the way my middle son looked than I did about being a single mom. It seemed no matter where I turned, there was another single mom going through the struggle just like me! If I'm going to be completely honest, I was actually talking to and yelling at myself.

I was ashamed of myself. *How did I end up in that situation?* I was a straight-A student in high school. I was accepted to a good four-year college. At the age of 18, I had a great job (for my age) making $10.00 per hour. I had my own car and was surrounded by a family that wanted to see me succeed in life – especially a mother who didn't want to see me become another single mother just like her. **So, how in God's creation did I, Ms. Jennifer Pink, become a single mother not once…not twice…but three times?** Every morning, I woke up yelling at myself. I tried to convince myself that I was worthy and more than just a single mom. I was still a child of God.

Maybe.

I think.

My Fight With God

I swore I left church because I was hurt by the people. They didn't love me when I needed love. I swore I was following God and striving for perfection, but as soon as I stumbled, *"God's people"* turned their backs on me.

Let me just cut through the crap right there…

I was in church to serve the **LORD** – *not* His people. I should have been seeking God's love and not that of His people…but I digress. I clearly didn't know that then. Looking back, I must be honest and admit I left church because I was ashamed of myself. My sin wasn't something I could hide at home. My sin wasn't something I could "take to the grave". The outcome of my sin was sitting right next to me in the pew! Everyone could see that I had sex outside of marriage. Everyone could see that my marriage didn't work. Everyone could see that I was a single mother of not one…not two…but *three* babies. I was ashamed because I knew the Word. I wanted to please the Lord. So, again: **How in God's green creation did I end up making this mistake three times?** That feeling right there…that **SHAME**…is why I turned my back on Jesus and why I kept making the same mistakes.

When I started working on some other things in my life, I was able to get to the point of being able to see and admit why I walked away from God. Like the good church folks say, *"Everything happens for a reason!"*

Well, I'm **pretty** sure this book is my reason.

Round Three – The Shame of it All

I have 'been there, done that'. I have now written a book about it so you don't have to 'go there or do that'. As you can see, I'm not biting my tongue one bit. I'm going to give you **all** of me – *raw and authentically* – so that you can learn the lessons taught to me…not the experiences.

Make note that I said **"lessons…not experiences"**. Later on, we will come back to that. For now, let me dig deep and share with you all about the shame I felt, put on myself, and the shame some familiar men and women of God have been through.

To me, the **biggest** sin I can think of is disowning Jesus. I know…I know…**I know**… Sin is sin in God's eyes. That statement isn't 100% true. If we're to be honest, we are humans and in our **minds** and **realities**, some sins are much worse than others. For example, lying isn't equal to murder. Stealing because we have hungry children to feed isn't equal to stealing for recreation. With that being said, I had to take a really hard look at myself and say, *"If Peter could disown Jesus not once…not twice…but three times in one night and God still loved and used him for His kingdom, then maybe I'm taking this shame of being a single mother a little too far."*

My Fight With God

Let's take a look at good, old Peter:

"Arresting Jesus, they marched Him off and took Him into the house of the Chief Priest. Peter followed, but at a safe distance. In the middle of the courtyard some people had started a fire and were sitting around it, trying to keep warm. One of the serving maids sitting at the fire noticed him, the took a second look and said, "This man was with Him!" He denied it, "Woman, I don't even know Him." A short time later, someone else noticed him and said, "You're one of them." But Peter denied it: "Man, I am not." About an hour later, someone else spoke up, really adamant, "He's got to have been with Him! He's got 'Galilean' written all over him." Peter said, "Man, I don't know what you're talking about." At that very moment, the last word hardly off his lips, a rooster crowed. Just then, the Master turned and looked at Peter. Peter remembered what the Master had said to him: "Before the rooster crows, you will deny Me three times." He went out and cried and cried and cried" (Luke 22:54-62, MSG).

I'm sure the story of Peter denying Jesus three times isn't new to you, nor is at least some of what Peter did in building the Church **after** his denial. It sure isn't new to me. I've heard it a million times used in various sermons on various topics such as how God still loves us and can use us after we sin, to how we are all wretched and sinful. For me, all of the sudden – in that moment when I was examining my own sin and feeling my own shame – I began to see and understood it for myself.

Round Three – The Shame of it All

The Bible never really goes into what Peter felt other than we see he went out and cried. If you are a single mother – whether because you and your husband didn't work out, your father's child was removed from your life via death or incarceration, or he was a dude you were seeing and it simply didn't work out – I can *almost* guarantee you have cried over your situation. We've all shed those "ugly tears" when the realization hits us that we are faced with the daunting task of raising our children without their fathers as a daily presence in their lives. If you haven't, you most likely haven't had a **real hard look** at your situation and the chips your children have stacked against them because they come from a single-parent household.

I'm going to go a *bit* further than what's written in the text of the Bible: I'm going to put **myself** in Peter's shoes. I am the one whose life has been completely changed by living to serve Jesus. I've been witness to countless miracles. I've seen Him raise the dead. I've heard the story about Mary's immaculate conception (*probably from Mary herself*). I know without a shadow of a doubt that Man **is** God in the flesh, and they are persecuting Him for no justifiable reason. He is my Friend, my Brother who they are unjustly and unfairly putting to death. I have **never** denied Him before. I have stood in protection of Him for many years.

Now, I can't even understand or imagine why not once…not twice…but *three* times I denied knowing Him, serving Him, and loving Him. I would have run off and had one of those "ugly cries" where the snot comes flowing out of both nostrils and I couldn't be consoled. I would have looked at everything I've done with that Man and doubted myself. I would be ready to take my own life and not live another day on this Earth because I've betrayed the **ONE MAN** who always had my back. I don't know if I would have been able to show my face at His crucifixion, let alone stand before Him after He rose from the dead.

Let me be nakedly honest with you: That is **exactly** how I felt when I was pregnant with my third child.

While pregnant with my first child, I was so ashamed, I left the church and wrote it off as *'I don't want to be fake'*. I walked around telling people I'm living in sin and that the Bible clearly states lukewarm is **not** the way to go. I chose to be cold for Christ.

> *"I know your works; you are neither cold nor hot. Would that you were either cold or hot! So because you are lukewarm, and neither hot nor cold, I will spit you out of my mouth" (Revelation 3:15-16, ESV).*

Round Three – The Shame of it All

I sought redemption with my second child; I married the father. Heck, we even went back to church and studied the Bible again. When the marriage ended, I used the mess as my excuse to go back to being cold. I was **so** determined to be cold for Jesus, I had my third child. During my third pregnancy is when God started opening my eyes and showing me that it was, in fact, the shame of my sin (*aka my **pride***) that was keeping me from God – not Him or His people. I'm pretty sure during my third pregnancy I felt almost exactly how Peter felt. I was looking back at everything I had done, accomplished, the people I had studied the Bible with and helped save, the 'counseling' I had given to so many in their times of despair, the child-rearing I had done up to that point, the relationships I was involved in, and thought it was all one big pile of crap that amounted to nothing.

I was a 28-year-old woman who (as they said) had her whole life ahead of her…making the same mistake for the **third** time. I had the real "ugly tears" and realization that I am the sole parent for these three little people and I've stacked the chips very high against them. The **only** difference between Peter and me was that it all happened in one night for him; for me, it took seven long, hard-lesson-filled years.

In essence, I like to look at it as I denied God's Word three times (*I'm sure the number was considerably higher, but who's counting all of that other stuff right now*). So, if God **still** loved Peter and **still** used him to save thousands upon thousands of people, then why would He not **still** love me and **still** use me to save others? Now, I'm not saying my walk is identical to Peter's. I want to make that clear. Throughout all the times I turned my back on the teachings of the Lord, I never denied He was Lord. I never denied knowing Him.

Why, then, do I hold my sin as worse than that of Peter's? (*I say "why do I hold my sin" because when you look at the truth of the matter, nowhere does the Bible say that my sin is worse.*) No one has ever opened their mouth to actually tell me I needed to put the 'Scarlet Letter' on my chest and should walk with my head down when I entered a church. *Why do I feel like I have to do exactly that?* Because I **believed** my sin was the worst thing I could ever have done in the world.

Let's take a look at Rahab the Harlot (*aka the prostitute*). We first see Rahab in Joshua Chapter 2 of the Bible. She was from the land of Jericho – a land that did not serve or honor God. She was known throughout Jericho as a Harlot…similar to what we would today call "the town slut". Yet something inside her caused her to not only take in two of God's people, but also hide them from the people of Jericho and the King who were looking to kill them because they were all afraid of the people of Israel.

Round Three – The Shame of it All

Let me pause right here in this story for a minute...

I'm not sure if you have caught on to the fact that I don't just have three children; all of them have different fathers. To make it plain, I have three "baby daddies". Although no one has ever said it to me directly, I used to walk around with this immense shame that people would think of me as a slut. I carried the shame so much that on first meeting me, I would be ready to tell people that all three of my children were products of long relationships and that I was married to my second child's father. I needed to make sure I removed people's possible preconceived notions of me and my situations. In all honesty, I'm pretty sure I went out of my way to serve and help people so they wouldn't view me as a situation that should be pitied and a woman who had no wits about herself and ended up with three kids by three different men.

I wonder if that was how Rahab felt in the moment when she took the two men of Israel into her home and hid them. *Was she in some way trying to right her wrongs or prove she was more than a harlot?* I ask you to take a second and ponder that thought. What are you currently doing in your life that is motivated by your need to prove you are more than "just his baby mama" and not "just another single mother"?

My Fight With God

If you continue reading in Joshua Chapter 2 Verse 8, you see Rahab go to the men of Israel and first declare that she and the entire city knows that the people of Israel are going to take over their land – Jericho.

> *"I know that God has given you the land. We're all afraid. Everyone in the country feels hopeless. We heard how God dried up the waters of the Red Sea before you when you left Egypt, and what he did to the two Amorite kings east of the Jordan, Sihon and Og, whom you put under a holy curse and destroyed. We heard it and our hearts sank. We all had the wind knocked out of us. And all because of you, you and God, your God, God of the heavens above and God of the earth below" (Joshua 2:8-11, MSG).*

But then she makes a bold move and asks God and the men to show her mercy and save her and her family's lives. Get this: God gives her – through those two men – exactly what she asked for:

> *"Now promise me by God. I showed you mercy; now show my family mercy. And give me some tangible proof, a guarantee of life for my father and mother, my brothers and sisters – everyone connected with my family. Save our souls from death!" "Our lives for yours!" said the men. "But don't tell anyone our business. When God turns this land over to us, we'll do right by you in loyal mercy"" (Joshua 2:12-14, MSG).*

Let's look at that closely.

You mean to tell me that a prostitute who doesn't know God, has never cried out His name in praise or admiration, cannot only be used by God, but can also ask God to spare her – and He makes a deal with her?

Round Three – The Shame of it All

I've clearly been going about this holding on to my shame thing all wrong!

You mean to tell me I don't have to be holier than thou?

You mean to tell me I don't have to walk around like I'm always dressed in God's whites and nothing is dirtying up my clothing?

You mean to tell me I don't have to pretend to be perfect (while having secret sins) in order to be used, protected, and given God's promises?

I can **easily** imagine you wanting to look at me cross-eyed right now. You can stop it right now because you know you've allowed similar thoughts to creep up inside of you! I'm sure, just like me, you have allowed the shame of what you've done and what you're doing to keep you from thinking and believing that God still loves you, that He can and will use you, and that He will protect you and keep you safe.

Rahab's story doesn't end there. When the people of Israel came to take over Jericho, Rahab, her father's household, and *everyone* connected to her were saved (you can read all about the account in Joshua 6:17-25). Her story doesn't even end there with God keeping His promise to her! If you study the lineage of Jesus, you see that He came from David – and that David's lineage came from **Rahab**!

So, to confirm: The **BIBLE** tells me that a Harlot – a prostitute and town slut – can not only be saved from destruction, but can also bear the fruit of God? Her legacy can far exceed her reputation of being a prostitute and she can forever be remembered as the woman who served a God she didn't even know but was saved by – and then able to bear the fruit that bore God Himself?

My question again is: *Why did I let the shame of what I've done and was doing keep me from trusting, walking with, loving, and serving God?*

Why are **YOU** letting the same thing happen?

Throughout the remainder of this book, we will uncover the masks, dig deep, and discover why we will never have to be ashamed again.

My Fight With God

ROUND 4

Josiah My Catalyst for Change

Round Four
Josiah: My Catalyst for Change

I **had** to be humbled. My pride **had** to be taken from me. God was building me back up and setting me up for following His plan for my life, but I never humbled out *completely*. I was blinded by what others told me I should be doing and what *their* vision of my life was.

God sent me *Josiah*.

When I had my first child, I gave her a 'J' name because I wanted her to be my mini-me. When I had my second child, I wasn't even ***thinking*** about giving him a 'J' name, but my daughter said to me, *"If he doesn't have a 'J' name, he won't be a part of the family"*, so I simply honored her wishes. I had dreamt of getting married again and wrote down **tons** of boy and girl names for my future children. I always struggled with the boy names because I couldn't find any that weren't being used by people in my family **AND** were Anglo-Saxon enough to be well-received by the world (yes, that's important to me).

My Fight With God

Then I got pregnant with my last baby. His father wanted to name him something awful that **didn't** start with a 'J'. All of the sudden, I wanted to name my son *Josiah*. It sounded like a biblical name, but I never heard of it and never looked it up. Many people **told** me it was in the Bible. My grandmother even gave me a framed picture of the name *Josiah* and its meaning, yet I **still** never knew what it meant. Even after I returned to church and had shared with so many people what a catalyst for change *Josiah* had been in my life, no one told me the story or said anything about his name. When I was finally ready, I started to feel God on my own. I heard His voice and He revealed to me that He had sent me *Josiah* all along.

According to the Bible, *Josiah* was the last good King of Judah. He was the catalyst for change in the people of Judah. He went on a path opposite of his father and grandfather. *Josiah* was broken when he learned that the people were not following God and that their disobedience was the reason for their destruction. According to 2 Kings 22 starting at Verse 11, *Josiah* ripped his clothes and repented immediately upon hearing of the laws the people had forsaken. He then went to be about His Father's business in restoring the people back to God.

Round Four – Josiah: My Catalyst for Change

When I learned and understood that story, I had chills and saw God like never before. You see, one thing I **immediately** understood from the story as I read it is that *Josiah* did the complete opposite of what those who raised and ruled before him did. Although he was young, he knew *something* was wrong and he needed to do something different. He immediately sought after God by rebuilding the temple (see 2 Kings 22:3). He had never even heard the laws, nor had he seen them, but he knew the temple needed to be rebuilt. From there, he found the laws and was immediately broken. He became the catalyst for bringing the people back to God.

Let me take you back to when I was pregnant with *Josiah*. I had experienced some of the lowest points in my life. When I was homeless, I had hope that it would work out. When I was jobless, I knew I would find a job…it was only a matter of time. When I was struggling to feed, clothe, and provide the basics for my two children, I was worried but knew my family would help. The welfare system was my safety net. **BUT**, when I was pregnant with *Josiah*, I doubted myself and felt like I was **exactly** who everyone said I was: **NOTHING**. I felt like I had ruined my life and that there was no way to fix it. Yeah, I had a job, a place to live, and some sense of stability, but I didn't have **me**.

I hid my pregnancy with *Josiah* from everyone except his father and godfather for the first four months. I finally told my mother at that time because I knew I couldn't hide it anymore. I lived in fear every single day of my pregnancy that I would lose my job, my home, my kids, and my stability. I couldn't explain to anyone why I thought those things, but I knew deep down inside that **this** baby was going to be the straw that broke the camel's back.

Josiah's father is the best example I can give of how low I had sunk. He was a man who had known me on and off for about 10 years. He knew my innermost secrets and insecurities. He knew I was so dependent on his love, I would do anything to get and keep it.

I had been around hustlers my whole life, but they always protected me and kept me **out** of the hustle because they said I was worth more than 'that life'. They cared enough about me to keep me **out** of the hustle.

Not *Josiah's* father.

I thought that because he showed me the ins and outs of his hustle and because he allowed me to be a part of his whole life, he really loved me.

When he had me meet him at the drug house to bring him food or his friend's kids groceries, I thought he trusted and loved me.

Round Four – Josiah: My Catalyst for Change

When he had me watch a drug deal go down and then watch them get caught, I assumed he wanted me to understand how the business worked in case I needed to help him out one day.

When he told me about having to go to the club every night in order to pick up new women so he could bust checks in their accounts, I wanted to believe that he was just doing what he had to do to get over and take care of his family.

When he had me meeting his Nigerian connects to pick up money orders and drop off ATM cards and whatnot, I told myself that it was okay because he was providing for my kids and me.

The **TRUTH** of it all was he **HAD** to show me everything. He **HAD** to make me a part in order to break me *completely* – in order to remove *any* love I had for myself. He **HAD** to strip me of my morals, self-respect, and good name so that I would follow him wherever he went…and so that I would see him as my god.

By the time I became pregnant with Josiah, that man had just about ***destroyed*** my life – and God was in the process of building it back up. Truth be told, *Josiah's* father was the reason I was homeless. He put my kids and me in a house and then one month later, decided he wasn't going to pay for it. He was the reason I couldn't get a bank account for quite some time. He had ruined my last accounts with his hustling schemes.

My Fight With God

When I broke it off with him, God blessed me with a job, an apartment, and a way out. I didn't **SEE** the blessings in the moment, so when I got back on my feet, I allowed that man to smooth talk me right back to the place where he last left me: his bed. Getting pregnant with *Josiah* doesn't end the story. His father begged me not to abort my baby. He showed me a man who was *excited* to have another child and promised to support me through it all. He wanted me to name my unborn son 'Sir Gabriel'. I thought, "How pretentious of him! It's not even a 'J' name!"

(I must admit, however: I almost named him 'Sir Gabriel'.)

Then, reality **slapped** me in the face. He publicly denied my child to another woman because he didn't want to lose the benefits she was providing him. In that moment, I knew my child was not to be named anything he wanted. Still, it didn't stop me from believing his lies and falling for his deceitful ways. When he missed **every single** doctor's appointment; when he wasn't there when I found out the sex and that I was having a big baby; when one of his **other** women texted me early in the morning because she had found out I was pregnant but he had again denied my child to her, I let it **ALL** go. I accepted his excuses and continued on.

In reality, I hated myself. I hated the woman I had become. My depression was at an all-time high, but I continued to smile. I continued to try to make it through.

Round Four – Josiah: My Catalyst for Change

When his phone was cut off days before I gave birth, I went to his home to reach him. At the door, he shooed me away. He didn't even open the door for me because he had another woman on the way. He knew he wouldn't be able to lie about *Josiah's* and my existence at that point.

I remember the day like it was yesterday…

I didn't fight, scream, or turn into the angry black woman that I could have…and wanted to. I simply turned around and walked away. I was already broken. There was nothing to fight for. My voice was already gone. What was I going to scream about? Did it hurt? **Yep.** Did I cry? **Yep.** But I had no clue how to stop the pain, end the frustration, and stop him from having the power to kill me from the inside out.

Three days after that brief visit, I went into labor. Labor has a way of bringing the rage out of you. *I'm sure all the women and men who have gone through the throes of labor know* **exactly** *what I'm talking about.* Well, before my labor got too intense, my rage exploded. I posted on his Facebook, which to him was something I was **NEVER EVER** supposed to do. I *think* I posted three or four public messages about how I was in labor, how I was at Cedars if he had time to come witness the birth of his child, and something else to the effect of his phone being off since he had lied to so many women.

Even then, God had His hands on me and protected me. Soon after my rage exploded, I found myself in full-fledged labor like never before. *Josiah's* birth was the one that **completely** changed my life. We all know by now that I've been through two other birthing processes. In comparison, they were easy…nothing an epidural didn't make better. With *Josiah's* birth, the epidural didn't take effect. I had to feel **every** pain and **every** push. When the man who fathered my child never showed up to the hospital or to see my son, I couldn't hide the shell of a woman I had become.

Josiah's birth is the **only** birth I can vividly remember. I remember cussing out the nurses. I remember not joking, laughing, or being sarcastic with the doctor. I remember wanting to kill his father. I remember almost breaking my mother and *Josiah's* godmother's hands.

After his birth, I remember feeling lost, hopeless, depressed, and like I should have given him to someone else because he deserved far more love than I thought I could **ever** give. I was filled with **so** much hatred – especially towards his father, who I couldn't help but to think of every time I looked at my son. The truth is that hatred was really towards myself.

Round Four – Josiah: My Catalyst for Change

From the very beginning, I knew my relationship with *Josiah* was very different than that of his siblings. He even looked at me differently than the other two had. There was this twinkle in his eyes that I couldn't explain. As much as I feared not being able to love him because of how much I hated myself for having him, when he looked at me, I would fall in love with him all over again. I know what I'm about to say may sound extremely crazy, but for the first time, I felt like a **MOTHER**. When I had Jocelyn, I was young. She was basically my baby doll/road dawg. I didn't coo and get all fussy over her. I made her independent, strong, and resilient *very* early. When I had Justin Christopher, his father's family was so involved, I had to **fight** to be a mother. To this day, I know I lost that fight weeks before he was even born – yet I still fight. Everyone who met *Josiah* instantly fell in love with him his first few months of life…even though many of them were against him being born. *Josiah* seemed able to heal my heart and touch my soul like nothing I had ever experienced and no one ever could.

I never wanted to be the reason why a man didn't have a relationship with his children. I never wanted to be the "Baby Mama from Hell" like I had heard about. So, even though I was hurt, broken, and just about destroyed by *Josiah's* father, whenever he wanted to see him, show him off, or talk to me, I obliged. He even bought fresh fruits and vegetables for me to make baby food, a toy or two, and some clothes a few times. I wanted him to have a relationship with *Josiah* so bad, I tucked away every ill feeling (*and my motherly instinct*) to let him 'play dad' whenever he wanted.

Although I am known for having over-the-top parties, I never threw them for any of my children's first birthdays. When I decided to take *Josiah* and a few family members to the zoo to celebrate his first birthday, I was completely shocked when his father said he wanted to pay for him to have a huge party at the zoo. Well, in an *effort* not to disappoint, he (of course) didn't pay for **that**, but he did pay for almost everyone to get into the zoo and he bought our lunches. He even invited some of *Josiah's* other siblings, including his sister (who is exactly one year older), her mother…and his new girlfriend. Now, although most women would have raised an eyebrow at the presence of the other baby mama or the girlfriend, I truly didn't care. I was just happy he was involved.

The other siblings nor their mothers would have never caused me to raise an eyebrow because they are, indeed, a part of *Josiah's* family. That girlfriend, though? Honey child, she was so much to deal with – but I did it! After the first birthday zoo fiasco, things between *Josiah's* father and I were okay…until I went and found myself a new man. I suppose some men really have that ideology, **"Once my baby mama, ALWAYS mine."** I, of course, thought the new man was the answer to all my problems, but I'll share more about him in a few.

Round Four – Josiah: My Catalyst for Change

Once Josiah's father got wind of the new man, he started acting funny. Eventually, we sort of stopped talking. So, a few months later when he requested our presence at his family's get-together so his father could meet all of his children, I eventually accepted the invite. What started as a seemingly innocent and potentially good meeting of *Josiah*, his siblings, and paternal side of the family turned into the final blow of humiliation by his father.

Josiah's father attempted to correct another one of his children's mother and me for what he considered rude behavior towards his girlfriend. I couldn't help but chuckle it off. There he stood: The man who had lied to so many women was **still** lying to so many people. The man who had denied his children to get over on women. The man who shooed me away from his doorstep just days before I gave birth – and he was trying to tell **ME** what was rude? I can only assume my chuckle struck a chord with him because his mood instantly changed from pleasant to contempt. He asked me a question that, to this day, I can't recall, but my response was something along the lines of, *"What do you expect when you build everything on lies?"* I guess my speaking **MY** truth and using **MY** voice was simply too much for him because at that moment, he dealt what he thought would be the final blow. He looked me in my face and publicly stated, *"If we want to talk about lies, we should talk about the fact that **Josiah** isn't my son!"*

My Fight With God

I admit it: I was at a loss for words. I didn't know what to say. *Was I being punked? Was this a joke? How could this man attempt to humiliate me like this in front of his family and my son?* What did I do in response, you wonder? Well, I picked up my son, turned to his **FATHER**, and said, *"If that's the way you see it, so be it. You will never hear from or see us again."*

I was only able to walk away and never look back because I had to protect *Josiah*. It was as if *Josiah* had given me the strength to do those things I was never able to do before.

The change didn't happen overnight. I'm pretty sure it is still happening a little more every day. After *Josiah* was born, there was a shift in me. It began to force me to see me the way God sees me. *Josiah's* birth didn't completely convince me or cure me of my lack of self-love issues. My story of not loving or seeing myself as the child of God I am was just beginning to show itself through my relationship with *Josiah's* father. Unfortunately, from the time *Josiah* was about 17 months up to two years old, I was in a physically-abusive relationship.

I had so many doubts that anyone would ever love me or accept me as a single mother of three with three different 'baby daddies', I began to grasp at any straws that were thrown my way. I went from a woman who wanted to be married and have a complete family, to a woman who was somebody's friend "with benefits". I no longer projected an image of someone you had to respect and approach even *halfway* decently. I projected an image of a woman who would take any piece of a man she could get. Well, that's exactly what I received!

Round Four – Josiah: My Catalyst for Change

Not long after I ended my 'friends with benefits' relationship (*deep down, I wanted and needed more*), I met a man. Now, the first impression was that the man appeared to be the one I wanted but thought was out of my reach. He showered me with attention, catered to my schedule, and was eager to help with my children. The levels of attention and affection he showed me were unlike anything I had ever felt before…but his life's scars were deeper than my own.

I remember the first time the abuse happened (*unfortunately, it wasn't the last*).

I was in the shower in preparation to take my baby to the doctor. He pulled the shower curtain back and asked me who the guy was on my phone. I know I must have looked at him like, "*Huh? What are you talking about?*", but he wasn't playing. He pulled me out of the shower and practically carried me to my phone that was in the bedroom. There was no one on the phone by the time we made it back to the room. When I figured out who had called and I explained it to him (*it was a co-worker wondering if I was at work yet asking me to bring breakfast*), my boyfriend wasn't having it. He slapped me, pushed me into the closet, and hit me a couple more times. After I picked myself up off the floor, I put some clothes on, put my kids in the car, and tried to hold it together as I took them to the doctor. He followed us and came into the appointment as if he had every right to be there.

After all of his apologies and promises to never do it again, I moved past it. I didn't tell too many people about the incident…and no, I didn't call the police.

Well, as I stated, that wasn't the only time he abused me. Every time that man hit me, kicked me, and punched me, it was *Josiah's* healing arms that kept me alive. Ultimately, my need to protect my children's lives made me value my own life and end the relationship.

When asked how I was able to get away, I respond with all honesty: *"When he was clearly ready to kill me and choked me to seconds away from my life ending, God stepped in and caused him to choke the life back into me. God woke me all the way up in that moment. I knew I was worth more, there was more to life, and I had children who deserved more."*

When that relationship ended, God really went to work on me through *Josiah*. Those were the days when I couldn't explain it to anyone, but all I wanted to do was cuddle with *Josiah*. I needed him more than I needed air to breathe.

It wasn't until very recently – before writing this chapter of the book – when I learned who *Josiah* was in the Bible. *Josiah's* name means **"Healed by Jehovah"**. *Josiah* is the man God used to bring His people back to Him.

In my life, *Josiah* is the child God used to bring **me** back to Him and to restore the woman God created me to be.

When people tell me how much *Josiah* and I look alike, I jokingly reply, *"I had to do it three times to get it right."*

My Fight With God

Faith of A Mustard Seed

Round Five
Faith of a Mustard Seed

So, you know how when you are going through life's ups and downs and all the church folk around you say, *"Have the faith of a mustard seed! That's all it takes!"*? Do you ever want to scream, **"That's just too much faith!"**? Well, I have definitely been that person. Heck, I'm generally that person every time I'm going through a big test, trial, or tribulation! It seems like during the hardest times, my faith levels are at an all-time low – unlike when things are going right and my faith soars!

Mentally, I get that a mustard seed is only one or two millimeters big – about the same size as the point on the end of a pencil. That's pretty darn small, but is (at times) **still** too darn much!

Faith is definitely a battle God and I have at least once a month. Sometimes, I'm ready for the battle. Other times, I'm so tired from the storm, I just say, *"But God!"* As Steve Harvey says, **"He ain't through with me yet!"**

Here are the lessons I'm learning about that *little* mustard seed of faith I need:

Faith means having **complete** trust or confidence in someone or something. *Complete trust? Complete confidence? What?* I'm at a loss. How on **EARTH** can I have *complete* trust or confidence? Trusting folks and having confidence in those around me is half the reason why I'm in most of the mess I'm in! I have all 10 fingers and toes in 20 different baskets because I don't have faith in any of this. The **first** thing God finally got through to me was that people were only telling me half the story. There's more to it than to *'just have faith'*.

"What good is it, my brothers and sisters, if someone claims to have faith but has no deeds? Can such faith save them? Suppose a brother or sister is without clothes and daily food. If one of you says to them, "Go in peace; keep warm and well fed", but does nothing about their physical needs, what good is it? In the same way, faith by itself, if it is not accompanied by action, is dead" (James 2:14-17, MSG).

When people were telling me to have the 'faith of a mustard seed', they weren't telling me that I couldn't just have blind faith and sit and wait for something to happen – which is what I **heard**. I also had to *do* something. See, for whatever reason, all I heard was, *"Just have faith. Just sit there and believe that God will make everything better."* Like for real? God is a magician and He will wave His wand and fix **this** mess? Seriously, if I have enough faith, things will magically turn around? Nope. Never happened. Not going to happen…at least not for me.

Round Five – Faith of a Mustard Seed

What they **should have** said (*or stressed*) was have faith that what you are doing will work out. Have faith that God will lead you in the right direction.

Now that I can actually begin to have faith in that, I feel like I'm doing something; I'm working towards a goal. I mean, they **should have** led with James 2:14-16 instead of some of those other passages of scripture they kept sharing. How about:

> *"Then Jesus declared, "I am the Bread of Life. He who comes to me will never go hungry, and he who believes in me will never be thirsty""*
> *(John 6:35, NIV).*

> *"Who is it that overcomes the world? Only he who believes that Jesus is the Son of God" (1 John 5:5, NIV).*

> *"Therefore I tell you, whatever you ask for in prayer, believe that you have received it, and it will be yours" (Mark 11:24, NIV).*

Or how about the famous mustard seed one?

> *"He replied, "Because you have so little faith, I tell you the truth, if you have faith as small as a mustard seed, you can say to this mountain, 'Move from here to there', and it will move. Nothing will be impossible for you"*
> *(Matthew 17:20, NIV).*

My Fight With God

See, those scriptures sound all nice and pretty, but let's be honest: I've prayed for **many** things and didn't receive them. I've told **many** mountains (*people, things, and actual mountains*) to move, and they didn't move an inch. The scripture in James really breaks it down: I can't just walk around talking about, ***"I have faith! Be gone, turbulent times!"*** I have to actually do some **work** to get rid of the situation. Now, don't get me wrong: I'm sure Jesus can fix anything He wants to fix at any time, but I'm also pretty sure He wants us to learn and work through some things.

The second faith lesson God and I fight about is getting through the tests and trials that come my way. I know there is a lesson in everything. I also know I'm not the wisest woman on the planet and have much to learn. But sometimes...***ohhhh, sometimes***...I just want God to write it down on a piece of paper in my language and that be the **end** of it. Going through all of these tests and trials sure does put a wrench in my faith muscle. Sometimes, I truly get *angry* with God and get to yelling and cussing (*I told y'all He ain't done working on me*) and crying out, **"WHYYY?"**

> *"Consider it a sheer gift, friends, when tests and challenges come at you from all sides. You know that under pressure, your faith-life is forced into the open and shows its true colors. So don't try to get out of anything prematurely. Let it do its work so you can become mature and well-developed, not deficient in any way"* (James 1:2-4, MSG).

> *"These tests have come to prove your faith and to show that it is good. Gold, which can be destroyed, is tested by fire. Your faith is worth much more than gold and it must be tested also. Then your faith will bring thanks and shining greatness and honor to Jesus Christ when He comes again"* (1 Peter 1:7, NIV).

Round Five – Faith of a Mustard Seed

God directed me to those verses. He wanted me to see, consider, and be content in knowing that the tests and trials I *feel* are killing my faith are actually meant to **produce**, **strengthen**, and **increase** my faith. It's like the old church saying, *"What was meant to kill and destroy you will heal and restore you."* I heard God's teaching about how my heart should feel when 'going through things' in my life, but I was still asking God, **"Why does it really have to go down like this? I mean, is this really necessary?"**

Then I remembered stories of other people in the Bible who had gone through **so** much worse: Joseph, Job, and the Israelites – just to name a few. I began to read, study, review, question, and try to analyze their situations in comparison to my own. I encourage you to study those stories for yourself, but I want to briefly touch on some in an effort to show you yet **another** lesson God keeps trying to teach me.

In the story of Job, we have a man who had everything: family, love, immense wealth, and prosperity. Nothing was wrong with him, so it seemed easy for him to glorify God. Then Satan was given *permission* to test Job. All of his 'riches' were taken away…**all at the same time!**

My Fight With God

"*Sometime later, while Job's children were having one of their parties at the home of the oldest son, a messenger came to Job and said, "The oxen were plowing and the donkeys grazing in the field next to us when Sabeans attacked. They stole the animals and killed the field hands. I'm the only one to get out alive and tell you what happened." While he was still talking, another messenger arrived and said, "Bolts of lightning struck the sheep and the shepherds and fried them – burned them to a crisp. I'm the only one to get out alive and tell you what happened." While he was still talking, another messenger arrived and said, "Chaldeans coming from three directions raided the camels and massacred the camel drivers. I'm the only one to get out alive and tell you what happened." While he was still talking, another messenger arrived and said, "Your children were having a party at the home of the oldest brother when a tornado swept in off the desert and struck the house. It collapsed on the young people and they died. I'm the only one to get out alive and tell you what happened." Job got to his feet, ripped his robe, shaved his head, then fell to the ground and worshiped: "Naked I came from my mother's womb, naked I'll return to the womb of the Earth. God gives, God takes. God's name be ever blessed." Not once through all this did Job sin: not once did he blame God*"
(Job 1:13-21, MSG).

I don't know about you, but **none** of my tests or trials have been quite *that* extreme or horrible. I may have lost a job; I may have lost my home; but I still had my kids and the ability to go out and recover those things I lost. Yet there I was, questioning God and asking Him **"WHY?"** over and over again. Then it hit me: Job didn't go through all that he did because he was bad or had done something wrong; it was all for **MY** benefit! Yes. I believe the Bible in its entirety is for **MY** benefit. God needed to show me an example of someone who was doing exactly what God called him to do and still be afflicted, all so I could learn about faith…learn how to make it through…and be able to share all of this with **YOU**.

Round Five – Faith of a Mustard Seed

The funny thing about faith is that we use it every single day, but we seldom pay attention to it until trouble shows up. Every day we have faith that we will make it throughout the day safely. We have faith that we will continue to breathe. We have faith that our families will return home. It's not until something happens outside of our expectations that our faith begins to waver and we doubt the Creator of all things. The main thing God has shown me in all of my faith battles with Him is that I have more faith in Him than a mustard seed, so I need to stop being scared and act upon it.

"No test or temptation that comes your way is beyond the course of what others have had to face. All you need to remember is that God will never let you down; He'll never let you be pushed past your limit; He'll always be there to help you come through it" (1 Corinthians 10:13, MSG).

"If you don't know what you're doing, pray to the Father. He loves to help. You'll get His help, and won't be condescended to when you ask for it. Ask boldly, believingly, without a second thought. People who "worry their prayers" are like wind-whipped waves. Don't think you're going to get anything from the Master that way, adrift at sea, keeping all your options open" (James 1:5-8, MSG).

All I have to do when my faith feels a little shaky is open my mouth and talk to Him, express to Him what I'm feeling, and tell Him what is going on. He will always point me in the right direction – whether it be through His Word, His people, or what I like to call "a direct download".

My Fight With God

Lessons I Need to Learn from Ruth

Round Six
Lessons I Need to Learn from Ruth

Before I committed myself back to the church, I was told more than once by more than one person that I am "wifey material". I treat every man I'm involved with the way I should **only** treat my husband. I give too much of myself to men who will never measure up to being my husband. Somehow, none of what they said ever really sunk in. It never went to my head and processed. I never carried myself like I'm God's gift to men, either. I'm pretty sure I needed some of that to happen, but we already talked about that.

When I **really** stepped into the church while looking for God to answer my questions and fix my problems, I started to hear how I simply needed to wait on my Boaz when it came to my desire to have a man. I was told over and over again how if I stay focused on being about **God's** business, He would supply me with my Boaz. That sounded great…until I met a man who was dressed up like Boaz, but was actually one of his **VERY** distant cousins (*we'll talk more about that in the next chapter*). What that situation taught me more than anything is that I actually needed to learn some things from Ruth before Boaz can come into my life.

Let's take a step back. I knew the *overall* story of Ruth and Boaz, but in all honesty, there is a **LOT** to the story that was never discussed or taught to me. The story I knew was this:

Ruth was married to Naomi's son. When he died, Ruth followed Naomi back to her land to take care of her so that she would not be alone. Ruth went out into the field to pick up scraps so that she and her mother-in-law could survive. While she was picking up the scraps in the land of Boaz, he noticed her working and inquired about her. He found favor in her because of her choice to support Naomi, her work ethic, and her humble spirit. When Naomi learned of this, she orchestrated the appropriate steps for Ruth to become Boaz's wife. Boaz loved and cared for Ruth. They bore a son who was definitely her blessing.

That's an **amazing** story in and of itself, but I've learned the Bible doesn't just give us pretty fairytales that we can hope and pray will happen to us one day. The Bible gives us stories that we should examine, study completely, and learn how to change our character in order to grow in God so that we can receive the blessings He has for us. There are so many important pieces to Ruth's story that I needed – and still need – to learn in order for my Boaz to find **me**.

Round Six – Lessons I Need to Learn from Ruth

First of all, Ruth wasn't "just working" when Boaz first saw her: she was committed, dedicated, and in true transparency wasn't worried one bit about finding another husband, having children, or anything else. She was focused on caring for her mother-in-law. That is definitely the first step in being the woman that Boaz requires. It's not just about being about our Father's (**God's**) business; it's about focusing on and taking care of what He has given us to care over. We have to be the woman, wife, mother, sister, and friend He has called us to be – whether or not we have a husband, children, siblings, or friends.

"But Ruth replied, "Don't urge me to leave you or to turn back from you. Where you go, I will go; and where you stay, I will stay. Your people will be my people and your God my God. Where you die, I will die; and there I will be buried. May the Lord deal with me, be it ever so severely, if even death separates you and me." When Naomi realized that Ruth was determined to go with her, she stopped urging her" (Ruth 1:16-18, NIV).

Ruth was determined to remain a good wife to her deceased husband and care for his mother as her very own. She left her family, her home, and everything she had known and grown accustomed to in order to fulfill her duties as a daughter-in-law – even though she no longer had a husband.

My Fight With God

When I take a gander back over my previous relationships, I was committed – but not **THAT** committed. I was married before and I wanted his family and my family to become one. I wanted to love them as my own mother, father, sisters, nieces, nephews, and cousins. The truth is this: They are the reason why I let my marriage go! I felt disrespected, ignored, and suffocated by them and their ways. If I'm to learn this lesson from Ruth, I must realize and admit: I wasn't a good wife to my husband. I didn't embrace and love his family. I wanted them to change to fit *my* ways, *my* views, and *my* standards. I definitely didn't honor my marriage now that it is over. I don't even speak to his family. I don't even care any longer – which shows I am not being like Ruth…and he was **not** my Boaz.

When I think about the way Ruth behaved, I now know that is the kind of love that is required of a wife. That is the kind of love I want from my future husband. To say the least, I think I am going to have to work on this quality…

Second, Ruth went out and found work to take care of her family. She didn't complain and didn't wait until they were in desperate need. She made sure they didn't go into need. She covered them from the beginning. Then, when she went out and found work, she was diligent, hardworking, and humble. Again, these are things we need to do when we get married. They are qualities I'm sure every man wants in his wife. Ruth wasn't sitting around waiting for Boaz to come get her and take care of her. She wasn't out complaining about the cards that life had dealt her. Instead, she went out and made it happen.

Round Six – Lessons I Need to Learn from Ruth

"And Ruth the Moabite said to Naomi, "Let me go to the fields and pick up the leftover grain behind anyone in whose eyes I find favor." Naomi said to her, "Go ahead, my daughter." So she went out, entered a field and began to glean behind the harvesters. As it turned out, she was working in a field belonging to Boaz, who was from the clan of Elimelek" (Ruth 2:2-3, NIV).

I've **always** went out and made it happen for my babies and me. I've **always** either had a job or been on a serious grind looking for one. I've **always** had a side passion, and when I really learned about business, I was able to take that passion and make a business. I'm **always** working on building wealth for not just my kids, but *THEIR* grandkids. The truth is I've always kept in mind that as soon as I got a man, I could stop or at least slow all the way down. I was always waiting for a man to come, take me away, and make all my troubles go away. In my mind, he would come, I could stop grinding, and just work. He would pay all the bills and I would worry about the extras I want my family to have. I never saw or thought of my role as the one who covers my family's needs. For me, I was only comfortable playing this role as long as I knew that someday, someone else would take it over.

It's clear to me now that I am functioning in my role. It is my job to care for my family at **all** times. It is my job to make sure their needs are met even before the need arises. If I am to be really honest here, I need to stop worrying about when Boaz is going to come in here and take over! When Boaz comes, I will still have to cover and care for my family's needs. I may not have to grind to fulfill those needs, but I will have to continue to grind for our future – just as I expect my husband to do the same.

Moving along…

This next thing I learned from Ruth was a little hard to swallow and come to terms with. The truth of the matter is our story does play a part in our future. Fortunately, it's not our whole life's story. I honestly believe we can, at any time, choose to change our story and make it different, but our story **does** matter. We can't say we want our Boaz, a man of God, a man who loves us to no end, when our life's story shows a woman who isn't worthy of such a man. ***Of course*** Boaz noticed Ruth when he looked out over his harvest! She was new and different – **BUT** what won his heart was when he heard of her work ethic and her character. When he met her, she was both humble and grateful.

Our own story tells the truth about who we really are. It's how others can tell if we are genuine, trustworthy, honorable, and respectable. Let's be honest here: We all put on our best selves when we are courting…and then soon after, our actions give off the biggest clues as to who we **really** are.

Round Six – Lessons I Need to Learn from Ruth

"The overseer replied, "She is the Moabite who came back from Moab with Naomi. She said, "Please let me glean and gather among the sheaves behind the harvesters." She came into the field and has remained here from morning till now, except for a short rest in the shelter." So Boaz said to Ruth, "My daughter, listen to me. Don't go and glean in another field and don't go away from here. Stay here with the women who work for me. Watch the field where the men are harvesting, and follow along after the women. I have told the men not to lay a hand on you. And whenever you are thirsty, go and get a drink from the water jars the men have filled." At this, she bowed down with her face to the ground. She asked him, "Why have I found such favor in your eyes that you notice me – a foreigner?" Boaz replied, "I've been told all about what you have done for your mother-in-law since the death of your husband – how you left your father and mother and your homeland and came to live with a people you did not know before. May the Lord repay you for what you have done. May you be richly rewarded by the Lord, the God of Israel, under whose wings you have come to take refuge." "May I continue to find favor in your eyes, my lord," she said. "You have put me at ease by speaking kindly to your servant – though I do not have the standing of one of your servants." At mealtime, Boaz said to her, "Come over here. Have some bread and dip it in the wine vinegar." When she sat down with the harvesters, he offered her some roasted grain. She ate all she wanted and had some left over. As she got up to glean, Boaz gave orders to his men, "Let her gather among the sheaves and don't reprimand her. Even pull out some stalks for her from the bundles and leave them for her to pick up, and don't rebuke her"
(Ruth 2:6-16, MSG).

My Fight With God

When Boaz actually spoke to Ruth, she immediately showed him the proper respect due him at that time. She honored him and submitted to her role as his servant, even though she wasn't. Her actions completely matched up to the stories he had heard about her. Now, let me say this before you get me confused with Ruth: In no way do I believe in servitude and mastership in today's time. It had its place in history. It was their way of life. I respect and learn lessons from it, but that is not how it is today. With that being said, there is a lesson here: The fact that we must have the same submission and reverence that is required – especially that of godly women towards godly men. You can't wait until you are married to become a submissive wife. You have to learn what it means to become submissive beforehand.

When I used to look back at my story, all I saw were my pitfalls, mistakes, and how horrible I was. I honestly never saw anything I would want a man to see and judge me by. The way I saw my past and myself is the number one reason why I don't have Boaz – and that's some real honesty right there. When I put my skewed lenses aside, the truth of the matter is that I wasn't learning from my past. I wasn't making changes to become a better me. I was simply repeating the same patterns and cycles over and over again with different characters. It wasn't until I started studying God for myself that the view I had of my past changed and I could actually learn the lessons He was trying to teach me all along. Only then could I start applying the lessons of Ruth and so many others.

Round Six – Lessons I Need to Learn from Ruth

There's a line in the song *Amazing Grace* that says, *"I was blind, but now I see…"* Well honey, **I was blind but now I see!** I **see** all the setups to greatness. I **see** all the times I made the right decisions – even when it was hard. I **see** all the lessons I learned so my Boaz won't have to teach me or wait for me to catch up. I **see** my worth! Now that I see all of those things, I am changing my story. I'm focused on the purpose God has put inside of me. I am dedicated to covering my family for *life*. I'm all about learning and living out His Word and plan for my life. I now understand Ruth's lessons and Boaz's heart. In all honesty, a godly man doesn't mind helping you grow in your character traits, but he probably doesn't want to teach you *everything*.

Boaz rewarded Ruth for her hard work, godly character, submissiveness, and respect by ensuring she had more than enough of what she was seeking. He didn't tell her what he had done – neither did he make a big spectacle about what he did for her. Basically, he did it in secret – and she was none the wiser.

I now know God will bring me my Boaz. My Boaz will do the same for me and it won't be about what everyone else sees or thinks, nor will I fully know all the ways he will protect and care for me.

My Fight With God

The last quality I needed to learn from Ruth that I **know** needs to be discussed and we can all learn from is the fact that she not only received advice; she took it! **Whoa, Honey Chile!** *How many women do that?* How many women seek advice from those who actually know what they are talking about – not their friends…not women who they think have it together – but from women who have been there, done that **AND** have the t-shirt to prove it? Here's the real truth: Ruth didn't even ask for the advice. She didn't ask Naomi what to do. Naomi offered unsolicited advice on what Ruth should do next with her life, and guess what? Ruth didn't even get mad about it!

> *"One day, Ruth's mother-in-law said to her, "My daughter, I must find a home for you, where you will be well provided for. Now Boaz, with whose women you have worked, is a relative of ours. Tonight he will be winnowing barley on the threshing floor. Wash, put on perfume, and get dressed in your best clothes. Then go down to the threshing floor, but don't let him know you are there until he has finished eating and drinking. When he lies down, not the place where he is lying. Then go and uncover his feet and lie down. He will tell you what to do""* (Ruth 3:1-4, MSG).

When God showed me that part, I screamed, **"JESUS, FIX IT!"** I have a hard enough time getting advice. I have a hard enough time opening my mouth and being 100% honest with what's going on and where I need help. For someone to come along and just **TELL** me what to do with my life? I don't know if I could handle that. I don't know if I'm ready for all of that, but I guess that's why it's *My Fight with God* - because we sure do battle it out!

Round Six – Lessons I Need to Learn from Ruth

So, not only did Ruth take that unsolicited advice, she actually *listened* to her mother-in-law – someone who was wiser and knew more than she did. She did **exactly** what Naomi suggested she do. Ruth didn't even question her as to why. She never asked, *"Why Boaz?"* I mean, Ruth never even said she wasn't happy with her life the way it was. She never even (according to scripture) mentioned wanting to marry again. Ruth had **no** clue if following Naomi's advice would make her happy, her life better, or if it was even going to work. She listened nonetheless because wisdom had spoken.

> *""I will do whatever you say", Ruth answered. So she went down to the threshing floor and did everything her mother-in-law told her to do"*
> *(Ruth 3:5, MSG).*

I am the **queen** of wanting to do things my way. I'm so polite and cordial when people give me their advice – whether or not I asked for it. Still, I almost always do whatever I want to do. When those with wisdom and discernment finally came into my life and said, *"He's not the one. He's not your Boaz"*, I responded, *"You just don't know him. You just don't understand."* Then, when he proved them right (**more than once**), I stopped talking and made it clear I did **NOT** want to hear what more they had to say.

You'll never guess what happened next…

Jesus had to go and sucker-punch me and let me learn all on my own. That particular breakup was the hardest because I truly believed he was my Boaz. I was tired and ready for Boaz, mainly because I knew I hadn't listened to the wisdom that God surrounded me with. I knew that mess was my own fault. My pride refused to accept all of those things.

Then there's Ruth...

Ruth is my example. She **DID** listen. She **DIDN'T** question and, in turn, she was blessed beyond measure. Ruth not only gained a husband; she had a son – the grandfather of King David! Talk about generational blessings! I know I want some of those things. I guess I better get in line and follow the example Ruth is setting for me!

> *"The women said to Naomi, "Praise be to the Lord, who this day has not left you without a guardian-redeemer. May he become famous throughout Israel! He will renew your life and sustain you in your old age. For your daughter-in-law, who loves you and who is better to you than seven sons, has given him birth." Then Naomi took the child in her arms and cared for him. The women living there said, "Naomi has a son!" And they named him Obed. He was the father of Jesse, the father of David"*
> *(Ruth 4:13-17, NIV).*

There are so many other pieces we could discuss in the story of Ruth and Boaz. We will definitely talk about Boaz in the next chapter, but I had to share with you those major lessons I learned and am still learning from Ruth as I prepare for my Boaz.

Round Six – Lessons I Need to Learn from Ruth

I didn't even touch on Ruth's modesty or the patience she exhibited because I didn't want to cloud the major lessons I needed to learn – those lessons I don't feel like anyone taught me…the lessons I feel get glossed over far too often…the lessons that will actually prepare me for my Boaz.

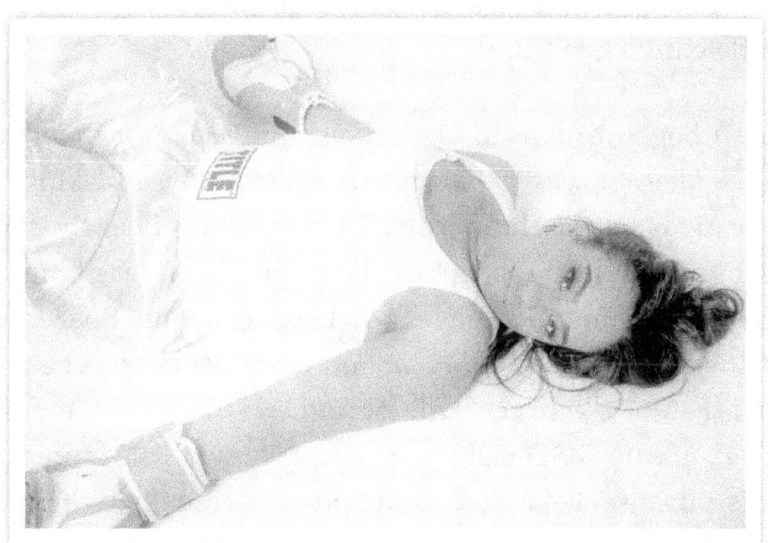

Who is Boaz? What Does He Look Like?

Round Seven
Who is Boaz? What Does He Look Like?

As a *SINGLE* Christian woman, I think a lot about my Boaz. In the beginning of my journey, I thought he was this mystical being (*so to speak*) that only Ruth and super-spiritual women could have. I didn't understand who he was, what he looked like, and how I would be able to identify him. No one was thoroughly explaining Boaz in a way that I could fully comprehend. Because of that, I knew this was a topic God and I were going to have to get clear on for this book – and for my complete understanding.

When I began to talk to God about **my** Boaz (*I'm going to be honest with you: I was 100% selfish in my talks*), I was asking Him where my Boaz was, how would I know he was Boaz, how long was it going to take to meet my Boaz, and what was I missing. In His own timing, God gave me clues to what my Boaz looked like. I was asking God for an *actual description*. Was he tall or short? Fat or skinny? Dark or light? Dreamy or average? Instead, in true **GOD** fashion, He kept showing me more about Boaz's purpose, behaviors, and spirit. Eventually, when I got out of the way and out of my feelings, I began to really listen and saw what God was showing me. I then knew exactly what my Boaz would look like.

However, in true **Jennifer** fashion, the fight between me and God was just beginning. I had to accept what He had shown me, which meant releasing any and everyone who didn't line up and, ummmm...well...that meant **EVERYONE** had to go because there will be only one Boaz – but he sure did have a *LOT* of cousins!

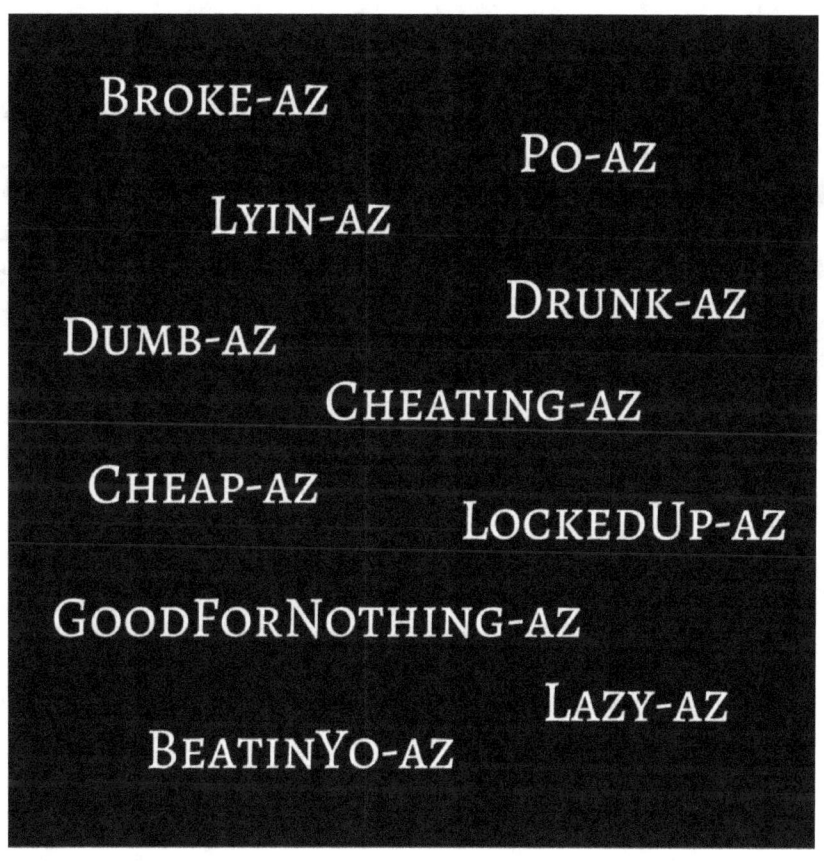

Round Seven – Who is Boaz? What Does He Look Like?

I'm going to share with you the revelations God gave me about my Boaz. All of them came from *studying* (which means more than **just reading**) the Book of Ruth in the Bible – specifically Ruth Chapters 2 through 4. All the while, I was begging God for true wisdom and discernment on the subject matter, which included listening to true men and women of God.

*NOTE: Please do **NOT** read anything else in this chapter if you aren't ready to know the **TRUTH**. Please do not continue if you are **NOT** ready to wait on **GOD**. I promise you this: If you aren't ready and you read on, you will be setting yourself up for some great inner-battles.*

First and foremost, when I was begging God to let me know what Boaz would look like, He showed me that Boaz would be the key to unlocking my destiny. Now, that is a very hard concept that many people get twisted. **Boaz will not give you purpose in life.** He will not save you from all your problems. He will most likely not ride in on a white horse and carry you off into the sunset. *(Sorry if I just broke your magic bubble. I know that news broke mine.)*

If you recall, when we discussed the lessons I learned from Ruth, then you know that we have to **already** be doing our work, living our lives on purpose for God, and seeking advice from those who are wise. The most important thing *(again)* is that we have to be doing our work! Boaz **IS NOT** the answer to your purpose in life. He is not going to magically give your life a whole new meaning. He will, however, come into your life after you are working the way you were born to work, after you have discovered the purpose for which God created you, and will be the one thing that can take you to another level in that purpose. Boaz will be the key to unlock the next level. That's not to say if you never get married, you can't be all that God has intended for you to be. If marriage is burning in your heart and you feel incomplete without it, then Boaz will be the key for you. He will be the one who challenges you, pushes you, and drives you to another level of purpose.

Round Seven – Who is Boaz? What Does He Look Like?

Now, because Boaz is the key to unlocking your destiny, that also means his purpose will be in alignment with yours. You will complement one another. If he has a purpose of farming and your purpose is more likened to building an empire, he *probably* isn't your Boaz. I'm sure right now you're thinking, *"There are many happily-married couples whose purposes aren't in alignment!"* That's true…which leads me to the next revelation: You can be happily married and **NOT** be married to Boaz! The two are not the same. This is where a lot of women and men get tripped up.

Let me explain what happens: They meet someone who is nice, cares for them, is everything they desire in the **natural** sense – and is almost everything in the **spiritual** sense. They get married, live happily ever after, and are perfectly fine – but that doesn't make him your Boaz…and that's okay. Think about it like this: *Everyone didn't marry Boaz;* ***only Ruth did***.

Most of us aren't going to do exactly what God wants us to do at every turn, so we may **NEVER** run into Boaz. For those of us who know deep down that Boaz is all we can have, this chapter is for you.

My Fight With God

I remember the dream I had before I even began my journey of living for God. In the dream, I was an amazing single mom champion. I spoke, taught, and fought for single moms. Then God showed me a man who was a champion for single fathers. Together, we went to a whole other level. We were able to bring so much healing and restoration to broken families. Our personal testimonies, relationship, and work all came together to unlock another level to both of our destinies. Like I said, this was **before** I opened myself up to God – before I even sought out spiritual mentors to get my life together. It was the most powerful dream I've ever had and one of the few dreams I can recall at any given moment.

God was showing me then what my Boaz looked like and what submitting to him would do in my life. Of course, I'm Jennifer. I fought that full submission thing and didn't want to believe the dream until I submitted to finding out who my Boaz was.

That is why I said to you if you don't want to know the **TRUTH** and are not 100% committed to waiting on God to bring you **YOUR** Boaz, then don't read this chapter. I know without a shadow of a doubt if you research Boaz for yourself – if you cry out to the Lord to reveal Boaz to you – He will give you a picture just as clear, which means you will have to let a whole lot of folks keep on walking…even ones you want to keep.

When I first thought about Boaz being the key to unlocking my destiny, it sounded good. Actually, it sounded **great**! More than anything, I wanted to go further in my dreams, business, and ministry. I envisioned one day being able to heal the entire family, not just the single mom.

Round Seven – Who is Boaz? What Does He Look Like?

That prompted me to start taking a deeper look at the men from my past, in my present, and even the men who were *trying* to be a part of my future. I became nervous, scared, and worried. I looked at the men I dated in the past – especially the ones I was in *LOOOOOOVE* with – and the ones I had children with. I knew **instantly** they never loved me because I never loved me. I never knew my greatness. I never knew I had a God-breathed purpose. That stung a little, but I brushed it off with, *"I'm not her anymore."*

Then, I started looking at the men around me – the men who I was entertaining as possible husbands; the men who possessed all the qualities normal people want in a mate. They were kind, loving, caring, supportive, and men who truly loved God…**BUT** none of them could ever help me unlock my destiny. They would never be able to walk this walk with me. They didn't have a passion. Their hearts weren't **bleeding** due to the state of today's families. That stung as well. I was sort of in a daze. I wondered why God would send me men who looked good on paper – **knowing** I'm longing for Boaz and **knowing** I would eventually come to the realization: they weren't the ones.

My mind began to panic. *What if I never find Boaz? What if I'm wasting all of my good years on mess?* You know, we women put these crazy dates on ourselves (i.e. I have to be married by age 30). Still, I knew it was God requiring me to have faith in Him and requiring me to put into practice all the things He had taught me. He needed me to stand up in my truth and not shy away from being bold in His promises. Eventually, I let all of those men go…all at the same time.

Wouldn't you know it? The men started coming in **droves**! I felt like I was under attack. I remember joking on Facebook several times:

WHO WROTE MY NAME ON THE BATHROOM STALL SAYING, "ADD JENNIFER ON FACEBOOK FOR A GOOD TIME"?

Seriously. Men were coming from *everywhere*!

My spirit told me, *"Be calm, ignore them, and focus on your work. If he is in the midst, he will make himself known to you."* I heard that over and over again. I stopped accepting Friend Requests from men who didn't have children in their profile, might be a potential client, or who I simply didn't know. For the first time in my life, I actually **stopped** looking and **stopped** making sure I was available for Boaz to find.

By the time this book is released, I'm sure I won't be married yet. For once, that is okay. For once, I know I'm doing exactly what God wants me to do.

Everything else God revealed to me about Boaz has to do with his character. Let's start at the beginning. What does Boaz mean? If you don't already know, you should know every name in the Bible has a meaning. They aren't named in the Bible 'just because'. The Hebrew word for Boaz means 'swiftness'. Boaz moves swiftly. He doesn't waste time. He doesn't weigh his options. He immediately does what needs to be done. God even shows us in His Word. The day after Ruth laid with Boaz, he went about claiming Ruth for his wife.

Round Seven – Who is Boaz? What Does He Look Like?

"Meanwhile, Boaz went up to the town gate and sat down there just as the guardian-redeemer he had mentioned came along. Boaz said, "Come over here, my friend, and sit down." So he went over and sat down. Boaz took ten of the elders of the town and said, "Sit here", and they did so. Then he said to the guardian-redeemer, "Naomi, who has come back from Moab, is selling the piece of land that belonged to our relative Elimelek. I thought I should bring the matter to your attention and suggest that you buy it in the presence of these seated here and in the presence of the elders of my people. If you will redeem it, do so. But if you will not, tell me, so I will know. For no one has the right to do it except you, and I am next in line." "I will redeem it", he said. Then Boaz said, "On the day you buy the land from Naomi, you also acquire Ruth the Moabite, the dead man's widow, in order to maintain the name of the dead with his property." At this, the guardian-redeemer said, "Then I cannot redeem it because I might endanger my own estate. You redeem it yourself. I cannot do it." (Now in earlier times in Israel, for the redemption and transfer of property to become final, one party took off his sandal and gave it to the other. This was the method of legalizing transactions in Israel.) So the guardian-redeemer said to Boaz, "Buy it yourself." And he removed his sandal. Then Boaz announced to the elders and all the people, "Today you are witnesses that I have bought from Naomi all the property of Elimelek, Kilion, and Mahlon. I have also acquired Ruth the Moabite, Mahlon's widow, as my wife, in order to maintain the name of the dead with his property, so that his name will not disappear from among his family or from his hometown. Today you are witnesses!" Then the elders and all the people at the gate said, "We are witnesses. May the Lord make the woman who is coming into your home like Rachel and Leah, who together built up the family of Israel. May you have standing in Ephrathah and be famous in Bethlehem. Through the offspring the Lord gives you by this young woman, may your family be like that of Perez, whom Tamar bore to Judah""
(Ruth 4:1-12, MSG).

Boaz will protect you more than he protects himself. Even when you sin, cause him to sin, and mess up, Boaz will cover you and make sure no one can ever say anything about you. Okay. So, to come to this understanding about Boaz, I first had to see something in the story I actually had never seen before. Naomi basically pimped out Ruth to Boaz. Naomi assumed she knew his character was righteous enough that it would all work out. It did, but what a **risk**!

> *"Wash, put on perfume, and get dressed in your best clothes. Then go down to the threshing floor, but don't let him know you are there until he has finished eating and drinking. When he lies down, note the place where he is lying. Then go and uncover his feet and lie down. He will tell you what to do"* (Ruth 3:3-4, MSG).

Now, that was deep in itself. It took me a minute to get over that revelation, as I'm sure it will do the same to you. You may be saying, *"But she just told her to lie down next to him."* I don't want to spend too much time here, but I will say this: If you look up Verse 4 in Strong's Concordance and look up the definition for the Hebrew words originally used for 'lie', you will see she was referring to **sex**. Naomi told Ruth to lift up Boaz's clothes and lay with him in a sexual manner! Ruth does as Naomi instructed and Boaz's response (*at first*) is, of course, **"Who are you?"**, but then he 'sees her' (*so to speak*) for who she really is. He says to her that the "kindness" she is showing is greater than that of before. He knows she is a woman of noble character and that he must do right by her and marry her.

Round Seven – Who is Boaz? What Does He Look Like?

> *"The Lord bless you, my daughter", he replied. "This kindness is greater than that which you showed earlier: You have not run after the younger men, whether rich or poor. And now, my daughter, don't be afraid. I will do for you all you ask. All the people of my town know that you are a woman of noble character. Although it is true that I am a guardian-redeemer for our family, there is another who is more closely related than I. Stay here for the night, and in the morning if he wants to do his duty as your guardian-redeemer, good; let him redeem you. But if he is not willing, as surely as the Lord lives, I will do it. Lie here until morning"*
> *(Ruth 3:10-13, NIV).*

Boaz doesn't send her away in the night. He also doesn't want anyone to see her and possibly think anything less of her than being the virtuous woman she is. He sends her home in the early morning hours – and he sends her home with more than she came with. Like we discussed earlier, the first thing he did was handled the business of making her his wife. He doesn't boast to anyone about their private moment. He doesn't even want anyone to know it happened – not because he wanted to keep her a secret, but because he wanted to **protect** her.

> *"So she lay at his feet until morning, but got up before anyone could be recognized; and he said, "No one must know that a woman came to the threshing floor." He also said, "Bring me the shawl you are wearing and hold it out." When she did so, he poured into it six measures of barley and placed the bundle on her. The he went back to town"(Ruth 3:14-15, NIV).*

Boaz took care of Ruth from the **beginning**. When he first saw her in the field gathering the leftover harvest, he made sure she had extra. When he had her sit at the table for lunch, he made sure she was full and had enough. When he sent her back home after the night they laid together, he gave her barley which, in their time, was food and currency. *Every single time Ruth was in Boaz's presence,* he was leading her and taking care of her. This is exactly who Boaz is. He will find you while you are working. He will lead you, take care of you, protect you, be swift in your relationship, and he will be the key to unlocking your destiny.

Deep, right? A real eye-opener – like I didn't know God was **THAT** real…did you? I'm going to be honest: When I understood what happened between Ruth and Boaz and how Naomi played her part, it was a saving grace. It was in that moment I realized even if I mess up, even if I don't hold tight to being celibate, even though I have laid with a man before, the **RIGHT** man's character will protect my name more than anything. Naomi knew Boaz's character and knew he would do right by Ruth. As such, I'm sure God knows **MY** Boaz's character and knows he will do right by me. Since I'm not God and He hasn't blessed me with a 'Naomi' up to this point, I'm going to have to ride on the side of caution and not lay down with any more men until we get married. **BUT** if I do, God has already given me the source of my grace.

Round Seven – Who is Boaz? What Does He Look Like?

Although I had to let **EVERYONE** go when I actually submitted to what God was showing me, I got excited! A new spirit of doing God's will in my life arose. I am eager to have Boaz walk into my life, but I'm even more excited and eager to prepare myself by submitting even more to God and by walking exactly in the purpose He has for my life.

I am also completely content in knowing that I am okay. I'm also noticing the men who do speak up and say something in a different way. Some don't get past the initial conversation because my brain space can't handle them. Some don't get past the first few conversations because it's clear there is no future. Every now and then, someone challenges, pushes, and forces me to grow. In every single one of those encounters, I'm growing into **exactly** who I need to be to complete my own task that God has set before me while growing into the exact helpmate I am called to be.

Who knows; maybe I have already met Boaz…maybe I haven't.

Either way, I'm excited to grow in **God**!

My Fight With God

My Fight Is Over But...

Round Eight
My Fight is Over, But…

I went seven rounds with God. We went toe to toe. Some rounds clearly lasted longer than others. Some rounds, I took so many hits, I thought my eyes were going to swell and someone was going to have to stop the fight by throwing in the white towel…but only I could end the fight. Only I had that kind of power. Well, I mean, I know God could have decided He was done playing with me and took me completely out, but I'm pretty sure He knew how the fight was going to end, so He just let me go through my journey.

"Whenever our hearts condemn us. For God is greater than our hearts, and He knows everything" (1 John 3:20, NIV).

God knew I was hard-headed, stubborn, a rebel, and determined to learn my own lessons – no matter how many ways out He gave me. He knew I needed a *complete* heart transplant and the only way my body wouldn't reject it was if He allowed me to fight Him. Only then would I really learn, truly grow, and be prepared for what's to come. Yeah, the fight is over, but the battle is just beginning – only **THIS** time, I'm not fighting God!

My Fight With God

When I decided to drop the gloves and lay them at the cross, I assumed, hoped, prayed, and wished that my fighting days were long behind me. I was so overjoyed to just be **done** with getting knocked down, **done** with not understanding, and **done** with making the same mistakes over and over again that I never looked at what might be laying ahead of me. I never once – *not even for one second* – counted the cost of completely surrendering and walking in God's will versus my own.

In case you haven't realized it, that is what the fight has been all about; me wanting to do me **my way** and fighting God because it wasn't working! All seven rounds could have been avoided had I simply consulted God first – back when He came looking for me when I was a teen. However, no matter what, no matter when I surrendered, no matter when I decided to let Him lead, I would have *still* had to grow into who He purposed me to be.

> *"For I know the plans I have for you, declares the Lord, plans to prosper you and not to harm you, plans to give you hope and a future"*
> *(Jeremiah 29:11, NIV).*

My fight has transitioned from wanting to 'do me' to learning how to be who He created me to be. I no longer have on my gloves and my smile shines brighter than ever. I've learned those lessons and have no desire to repeat a single one. I have completely and totally surrendered my life to God...and my true battle is just beginning.

Round Eight – My Fight is Over, But…

Today, God and I often have conversations like this:

Me: "So, ummmmmm, God; about that thing you keep asking me to do…?"

GOD: "Yes, Jennifer…?"

Me: "So, yeah… How exactly do I do that? Can I get a step-by-step guide? Can you make it be completely successful? Can you remove all of the obstacles that will stand in my way? Can this be very, very easy?"

GOD: "I've already given you the blueprint. I put it inside of you when I made you. You are already successful and no weapon formed against you shall prosper. And you already know I'm not the one who makes it difficult… It's really easy, if you ask me."

Me: "Look here, Jesus: You know I'm truly a special soul. You already know what I struggle with and how **NOTHING** is ever easy. And yeah…you put the guide in me – but sometimes…just sometimes…I have a hard time pulling it out. If you could just write it down **AGAIN** in plain, simple English, I *promise* to do just as you say and we can move on."

GOD: "Chile, you are truly **SPECIAL**. I made you that way. All I want you to do is walk in the purpose I created for you. Help the women who need you. Turn your struggles, fights, and pains into the greatness I have put in you. **Stop** all this foolishness and dragging your feet. ***Get to work!***"

Me: "For real, for real? That's how you gonna do me, Jesus? You just gonna call me 'special' and tell me to do the work you have called me to do? Alright, Jesus. I'm gonna go do what I think I should be doing and I'll be back to finish this conversation later. I just can't **DEAL** with you right now."

GOD: "Alright, then. I'll be here whenever you need to talk."

Me: "Yep – and don't say *anything* else because you know I like to have the last word!"

GOD: "Amen."

Me: "*JESUS!!!*" (*I take a long breath and roll my eyes...a **LOT**.*) "Amen."

GOD: "SHALOM!!!"

My fight is definitely over, but the battle and the work are just beginning. Now I'm going to have to learn how to walk in the purpose for which He created me. I'm having to do His will and not my own – daily. Writing this book was definitely a part of the battle and the work I am doing. I dragged my feet, hid my head in the sand, and tried to play the Lord by writing another book. He, being the smarter of the two of us, forced a ministry out of that other book. No matter how much I try to shake it, give it away, or ignore it, that ministry is my heart. That ministry is the reason I go so hard. That ministry is **ME**. No matter how many times I have those "Jesus praying in Gethsemane" moments and tell Him:

Round Eight – My Fight is Over, But...

"Father, if you are willing, please take this cup of suffering away from me. Yet I want your will to be done, not mine" (Luke 22:42, NLT).

He doesn't take the cup.

He doesn't let me just live the rest of my days in a resting place. He commands me to do the work He created for me to do. He demands that I walk in His purpose every single day. Now, that may sound easy or maybe it sounds like I'm ungrateful because I'm telling you how hard it is and how much work it requires. I can guarantee you: **BOTH** of those things aren't true.

It is far from easy because every single day, I have to die to myself. I have to *choose* to become more and more like Jesus. I have to write books like this that tell all of my business while leaving me completely naked and exposed so that another woman can begin to heal. I do it all for the sole purpose of helping another woman end their fight sooner, learn the lessons a little bit faster, and, most importantly, grow in Him daily.

I am far from ungrateful. I appreciate the wisdom I've gained. I appreciate my journey because it has brought me to this point in my life. I thoroughly appreciate Jesus dying on the cross for me to be able to fight with God and come out victorious on the other side - the other side of where I am today where it was very hot and not so pretty. Despite my gratitude-filled heart, despite my fight being over, and despite the fact that I am in a place of complete peace and joy, I still have to make the decision daily to live out His greatest commission for all of our lives – but in the way **HE** has commanded me to do it.

My Fight With God

"Then Jesus came to them and said, "All authority in Heaven and on Earth has been given to me. Therefore, go and make disciples of all nations, baptizing them in the name of the Father and of the Son and of the Holy Spirit, and teaching them to obey everything I have commanded you. And surely I am with you always, to the very end of the age"
(Matthew 28:18-20, NIV).

The Great Commission He has given to all who choose to follow Him is a hard task in itself: To go out into the world and teach them to **OBEY** all of the commands Jesus has given us. To be a part of people's transformations and teaching them to become new and become disciples of Jesus is not an easy-take-lightly task. You will be mocked, ridiculed, looked down upon, persecuted, and hated simply because **HE** was when He did it. It will be no different for you or me. You will want to give up and quit, but you can't because **HE** never did.

God didn't call me to just fulfill His Great Commission; He called me to do it in a very special and unique way that only I can. He gave me a unique purpose that no one else can fulfill except me. He charged me with being a mirror – a completely transparent and naked woman – so that others may believe in His power. He has called me to be ***Ms. Jennifer Pink, Single Mom Sage*** – the minister, mentor, author, speaker, and sister to single mothers who are hurting and in desperate need of Him.

Round Eight – My Fight is Over, But...

In order to fulfill His purpose in my life, I have to constantly grow. I have to constantly get closer to Him. I have to block out those who don't understand and leave behind those who can't handle the pink lights that shine from the inside of me. Some days, the burden is heavy. Some days, I feel so alone. Some days, I'm confused. Some days, I just want to be plain, old Jennifer. Some days, I feel so misunderstood and persecuted, I just want to quit and never look back.

I struggle with waiting for my Boaz – not just because I want God's best for me, but also because I know that my waiting will save so many other women. I know that every choice I make, every time I stumble, every hurdle I overcome, every time I fall, and every time I get up is not just for me anymore, but for every single woman God has assigned me to help heal. I am their gateway to Him. I am their picture of what it can be if they give up the fight and lay the gloves at His feet. I am the answer to their prayers and that, my friend, is an immensely difficult and never-ending job that causes me to **still** be on the battlefield.

My Fight With God

"Finally, be strong in the Lord and in His mighty power. Put on the full armor of God, so that you can take your stand against the devil's schemes. For our struggle is not against flesh and blood, but against the rulers, against authorities, against the powers of this dark world and against the spiritual forces of evil in the heavenly realms. Therefore, put on the full armor of God, so that when the day of evil comes, you may be able to stand your ground, and after you have done everything, to stand. Stand firm then, with the belt of truth buckled around your waist, with the breastplate of righteousness in place, and with your feet fitted with the readiness that comes from the gospel of peace. In addition to all this, take up the shield of faith, with which you can extinguish all the flaming arrows of the evil one. Take the helmet of salvation and the sword of the Spirit, which is the Word of God. And pray in the Spirit on all occasions with all kinds of prayers and requests. With this in mind, be alert and always keep on praying for all the Lord's people" (Ephesians 6:10-18, MSG).

My cup is full. The battle is far from over. My work is nowhere near finished, but…

I've put on the full armor of the Lord. I seek His face daily and listen to His voice constantly. I lay myself before Him, no matter what wrong or right I've done. I am no longer fighting. I've made the choice to put my gloves down. I now choose to live His will and not my own. I choose to **THRIVE** in Him every day, every hour, every minute, and every second He gives me breath to breathe. So, although there are hard times and storms raging ahead of me, I fear none of it because I know He is by my side and will guide me the rest of the way home.

My fight is over, **BUT** the battle has just begun.

I am glad to be on this side of the war.

Are You Ready to End Your Fight?

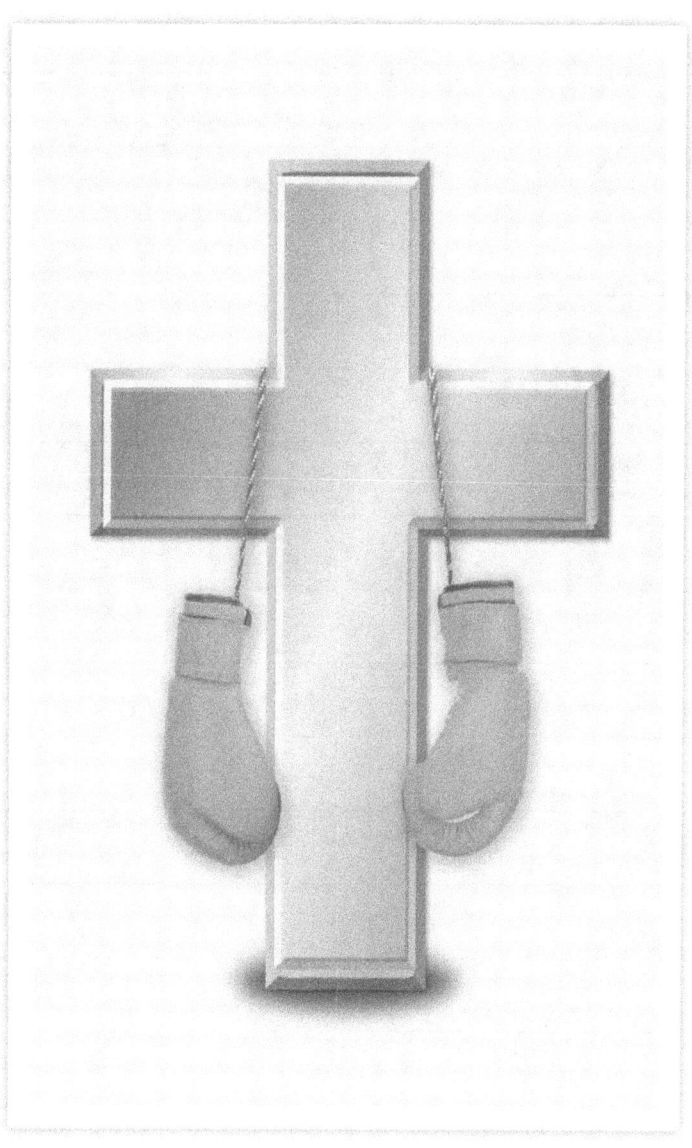

Are You Ready to End Your Fight?

My Fight With God

Are You Ready to End Your Fight?

My Fight With God

Are You Ready to End Your Fight?

LET'S GET SOCIAL!
CONTACT MS. JENNIFER PINK!

For more information about Ms. Pink, please visit:
www.msjenniferpink.com
www.facebook.com/msjenniferpinksms

For direct contact or inquiries, please email:
assistant@msjenniferpink.com

J Village, Inc.
Teaching & Creating Generational Wealth

www.ingramcontent.com/pod-product-compliance
Lightning Source LLC
Chambersburg PA
CBHW071523080526
44588CB00011B/1543